Trading on the
Seattle Merc

Trading on the Seattle Merc

David R. Capasso

John Wiley & Sons, Inc.

New York • Chichester • Brisbane • Toronto • Singapore

Library of Congress Cataloging-in-Publication Data:

Capasso, David R., 1958–
    Trading on the Seattle Merc : how to trade forward contract options
on the Seattle Mercantile Exchange / David R. Capasso.
    p. cm.
Includes index.
ISBN 0-471-06326-6
    1. Seattle Mercantile Exchange. 2. Nursery stock—Washington
(State)—Seattle—Marketing. 3. Commodity options—Washington
(State)—Seattle. I. Title.
HG6049.C24 1995
332.64'4'09797—dc20   94-31676
                                                              CIP

Printed in the United States of America
10 9 8 7 6 5 4 3 2 1

To my children, Shannon and Russell,
who make it all worthwhile, a center.

To AMK, whose unique motivational style was compelling,
had only patience been a virtue.
Dream not of today.

And to entrepreneurs, who toil day after day
to make a better life for themselves, their families,
and society as a whole.
Because of our aspirations and tolerance for risk,
capitalism survives.
To the naysayers we encounter daily,
the day we stop dreaming
is the day the system ceases.

Preface

Trading on the Seattle Merc is an introduction to trading forward contract options on the Seattle Mercantile Exchange (SME). Options can be viewed as an insurance policy; they allow the various industry segments to insure against the risk associated with maintaining inventory as well as price movement and future nursery stock supply. Although options and forward contracts, in a centralized trading market, are new to the nursery industry, their use dates back some 800 years. Contracts for delivery of a commodity at a future time and place were originally developed to improve trade throughout Europe and later used to stabilize price and efficiency of Japan's rice trade. In the United States, not until the middle of the nineteenth century did contracts to promote market efficiency within agriculture come into use.

From soybeans to heating oil, pork bellies to currency, no other mechanism for conducting trade efficiently has made a more positive economic impact for commerce, or for managing risk, than the introduction of forward markets. Exchanges are now sophisticated networks where buyers and sellers meet to discover price and, perhaps, profits. *Trading on the Seattle Merc* was written to assist the nursery professional (commercial hedger) who seeks to gain from this exciting and often rewarding mechanism, the forward market.

Options, as they are known in the financial world, are derivatives. This term is used because an option's value is derived from the value of the option's underlying product. The value of a stock option, for example, is determined by the value of the stock underlying the option. As the stock's price rises and falls, the option's value (price) follows in tandem. An SME option's value is determined by the underlying value of the product, trees. Therefore, as the value of the trees increases or decreases on the cash market, so does the option's value. An option unto itself has no value; its underlying product is the determining factor.

This book, written for the novice to forward contract and option trading, is the first published for the nursery industry. As the Seattle Mercantile Exchange evolves and trading of options becomes the industry norm, many financial books will follow. It is my hope that readers find this text informative and the products of the exchange helpful for their daily conduct of business. Although many concepts presented may seem new and foreign, the principles are basic business fundamentals. What may seem like complicated theories and hypotheses are merely analyses, reduced to writing, of business situations encountered daily.

If you are not used to analyzing complex formulas and data, do not be alarmed; the concepts can often be confusing, even to those with experience in the field. The message, however, should be clear: The nursery industry needs the efficiency that a forward market offers. If you come away with just that understanding, then the book has accomplished its goal: to inform the industry that business as usual does not have to be the future. If you are willing to learn, new ideas and concepts to resolve age-old problems are available.

Now, however, it is entirely up to those within the industry to educate themselves. Each reader will come away with his or her own opinions regarding the usefulness of a forward market. Only you can determine if the products offered by the exchange can assist with your operations. This book offers an opportunity to draw an educated and intelligent conclusion. Its purpose is to give basic information needed to evaluate options and their use in your business. To develop a rational opinion you need information; without it, any opinion is based merely on emotion. Emotion should certainly not rule the way business is conducted.

This text is written to give the reader a working knowledge of SME, the benefits of a forward market, and the use of forward contract options to secure inventory, for either price and supply hedging or speculating. SME's primary trading clients are "commercial hedgers," which consist of all segments of the nursery industry who are seeking to offset risk. This text is by no means intended to satisfy all trading strategies; it is an introduction to option trading and SME. It offers commercial hedgers an inside look at a forward market and shows how to benefit from the various hedging opportunities.

Many books are available that offer sophisticated option trading strategies, but unfortunately none is specifically written for SME contracts. Therefore, given that SME is in the early stage of development, it will be some time before financial authors introduce their strategies for successful SME contract trading. However, two books currently on the market might be insightful: *Getting Started in Options*, by Michael C. Thomsett, and *Option Market Marking*, by Allen Jan Baird (both published by John Wiley and Sons). In the meantime, SME member brokers are well trained and informed, and their sole purpose is to assist individuals to make the wisest possible market decisions.

Prior to starting this text, review the glossary to become familiar with the words and terms used to explain the forward market and related contracts.

SME was structured so that participants in the market have confidence that the exchange and those companies involved, such as growers, brokers, buyers, and sellers will perform. As this book outlines, every element of the forward market has been built to support and encourage that confidence. From the growers selected to the brokers and underwriters, SME has addressed every conceivable issue to ensure the financial integrity of the market.

One overriding factor for the development of any exchange has been to bring confidence to the industry that lacked confidence in their cash market transactions. Canceled orders, slow pay, or no pay are more frequent occurrences today then at any other time in the history of the nursery industry.

In addition, the material standards issue must be addressed. One of SME's purposes, at least for the plants traded on the exchange, is to give buyers confidence that the product received from SME is of the highest quality. Once a trade is made SME's obligation is to the buyer. Therefore, it is of the highest priority that any grower participating with SME produces the highest quality product. If they don't, their material is not accepted onto the market. Moreover, every tree to fulfill a forward contract has identical characteristics, be it height, width or caliper. This book explains in detail the process to ensure material consistency and related guarantees.

In my many conversations with industry individuals I have heard over and over how buyers are concerned about quality, and rightfully so. This concern, however, stems from the lack of confidence buyers have with the current process. I have been asked, for example, given that landscape architects like to tag trees, how will that be possible with SME contracts?

First, the only reason landscape architects, or for that matter anyone within the industry, tag trees is because buyers don't trust that the seller truly considers the buyer's interest. If buyers had confidence that sellers were concerned there would be no need to tag for material consistency. Certainly there will always be a need to tag, particularly for artistic appreciation, but not for consistency issues.

Second, for various reasons, this industry is beset with distrust. Therefore, SME has set the standards for material being traded and the industry over time will gain confidence that material traded on the exchange will consistently meet or exceed those set standards. Gone will be the days when the truck is unloaded and 60–70% of the order is acceptable.

Finally, in response to one naysayer, who, in a matter-of-fact cynical tone, when I informed him that the industry had more financial risk on the cash market than with trading on SME, he replied, "With commodity exchanges, for every winner there is a loser." The loser is the inefficiency inherent in cash market transactions. If the loser can be quantified, they are those that benefit from operational costs associated with maintaining excess inventory, marketing costs for product that doesn't sell, losses associated with spoilage and last but not least, the banks that are financing that excess inventory and the overall inefficiency within the market. Simply stated, inefficiency is the loser.

The point is, something needs to be done to remedy these industry-wide problems. A commodity exchange operating within the industry, whose purpose is to promote consistency and standardization as well as market efficiency, is a step in the right direction.

The history and function of exchanges, and the issues they resolve, are discussed in Chapter 2. Using this information as your basis, the subject matter that follows will be easily understood. It is imperative that the industry develops confidence in the forward market—a proposition to which all involved with SME are committed. With the support of the industry, many obstacles currently associated with cash market transactions can and will be overcome.

The building of the structure of the exchange took 2 years of often trying times. This book documents what that time represents. Although 200 years of exchange history and experience were available to serve as a model, integrating the best possible proven concepts and workable solutions to serve the economic needs of the nursery industry was quite a task.

Given that financial data, market analysis and other important historical economic information pertaining to the nursery industry was virtually nonexistent, useful economic models had to be built. Very little economic data, to say the least, has been written and/or studied regarding the nursery industry. With the advent of the Seattle Mercantile Exchange, this situation will change.

The various state associations that were contacted for economic information, other than stating that the nursery business was cyclical, had little to offer. Interestingly, most were cynical and viewed the usefulness of a forward market with skepticism. We found in the early research-gathering days that members of the various associations (growers, contractors, wholesalers, garden centers, etc.) contacted, whose hard work built this industry, were more intrigued by the idea than the associations whose members' interests they are paid to represent.

Among some individuals within the associations, there seemed to be a prevailing attitude that if they did not think of it, then it does not have merit. Certainly, many programs developed over the years by the associations were just, and many dedicated people were and are involved. However, what the industry needs now are solutions to problems, irrespective of who thinks of them. These solutions must strengthen and build on the foundation of the industry's financial structure. New twists on old ideas are not solutions, they are merely tools by which problems are masked.

As is the case with many tightly knit self-regulated industries, the association leadership often has self-serving objectives. It seems they are often more concerned with protecting their domain than with venturing out in search of true meaningful answers. This general sentiment, incidentally, was echoed by many members and former members who were interviewed by SME. Interestingly, many of the association's leadership were consumed with the notion that SME sought their association's endorsement. On the contrary, we seek to educate. Many were afraid if they took a positive position regarding the exchange it might be misunderstood by the members. The unemployment fear is overwhelming; thus, it becomes a catch-22.

I once had a conversation regarding the North American Free Trade Agreement (NAFTA) with a high-ranking nursery association official. With the impact of NAFTA and increasing numbers of products coming from Australia, New Zealand, and soon China, the U.S. nursery industry, as we know it, is about to change drastically. As the industry becomes "global," a forward market to improve efficiency within the United States will become more relevant than previously. If the industry, and in particular the growers, are going to compete and survive, status quo is not a prudent course.

> "Well," he said, "our association will fight to keep foreign product out."
> "So said other U.S. industries, such as electronics, banking, clothing, and so on—a very long list indeed," I replied.

Unfortunately, this is a naive way of thinking. Statements such as, "Let's not find solutions to the problems; let's lobby government," may excite and rally members around a cause, while directing blame to others. But when container stock starts washing up on U.S. shores, remember that this person merely changes employment and begins gins his rhetoric for another industry's association.

Whatever the reason, if your association needs assistance to understand how SME can assist its membership, please feel free to contact the exchange or a member directly. SME has many programs structured to further the education process.

The point, however, is that we must all do our part to strengthen the foundation on which the nursery industry stands. The Seattle Mercantile Exchange is but the first step in this regard. I trust you will receive the same experience and education reading this book as I received writing it.

STRUCTURE OF THE BOOK

Chapter 1 offers the reader a behind-the-scenes look at how the exchange was built, from the idea to the opening. From selection of genera and species to the development of the contracts traded, this chapter builds the basis for the forward market. Chapter 2 explores the history of contract development. Forward contracts have played an intricate role in the expansion of the world's commerce from medieval Europe to the futures markets of today. This chapter gives the reader an opportunity to fully understand the origin of contract trading. Chapter 3 outlines the exchange structure and defines, in detail, options and forward contracts. In addition, it covers strike prices, commodity types, and the necessary tools of trade. Chapter 4 looks at the cash market and the role it has played within the industry. Also discussed are historical cash market pricing and the dynamics of the cash market. To support the forward market pricing structure, historical price analysis is featured.

Chapter 5 details the cost associated with developing and carrying nursery stock, a term referred to as *basis*. Basis considers all expenses associated with nursery stock, such as labor, land, and carrying costs. Without a thorough understanding of the cost structure for growing and holding inventory, profitability is elusive. Chapter 6 shows how to use the forward market for hedging. The strategies outlined are developed from working examples and actual models built specifically for nursery stock. From using options to securing inventory to trading options, this chapter covers the principles behind hedging.

Chapter 7 offers a thorough understanding of how the forward market works. The relationship between marketing and pricing is discussed, as is the performance of the forward market. Chapter 8 details forward market pricing. How are trees, the product of the forward contract, priced? The impact of cash market pricing over the forward market is explained in detail. This, more than any other chapter, goes to the heart of, and offers the fundamentals of, forward market pricing. Chapter 9 explains option pricing. Options are derivatives, and as such, their value is determined by the value of the underlying forward contract. This chapter reviews the pricing logic and value determination of an option step by step.

Chapter 10 features various trading strategies, from buying and selling call options to buying and selling put options, in addition to buy and sell strategies. This chapter explains underwriting, from covered to uncovered writing and the principles behind each, as well as the best strategy for various segments of the industry. The book ends with final thoughts about the industry and the role of the forward market within the industry. An appendix of useful services and products, from software to books and magazines, is included to offer readers tools for their education of the forward market.

With the introduction of an exchange to the nursery industry, a new industry has emerged and a new market for exchange-related products and services has formed. The industry will need education, trading assistance, and so forth, and many companies that never thought of the nursery industry as a market for their products will begin to emerge. New ideas will be introduced, news ways of conducting business will be developed, and, more important, new money will be circulated. In the final analysis, the purpose of the Seattle Mercantile Exchange is the betterment of the nursery industry.

As with anything new, education is the important first step in the building process. John Wiley & Sons has made a commitment to assist with the education process. Let us hope that others within the industry come forward with material to support the long-term education needs of the industry. The various associations must get involved with educating their members, as must the business press within the industry. A strong and industry-supported forward market helps everyone. Those who plan to wait and see do a disservice to themselves, their companies, their members, and the industry at large.

With the help of many dedicated people from within the nursery industry and from others with exchange experience, SME officially began trading in February 1994.

Seattle, now that the Seattle Mercantile Exchange exists, has become the financial center for the Northwest nursery trade and serves as the developing center for the U.S. market. Like Chicago and New York, Seattle can be counted among those cities having a commodity exchange.

Acknowledgments

Many people are involved with the production of a work like this. One such individual is David M. Leonhardt. David had just completed his first year of M.B.A. studies at the University of Washington when I hired him as a research assistant in the summer of 1992.

With an undergraduate degree in aeronautical engineering and the brashness of a budding M.B.A., David spent countless hours arguing the why and how of SME. Without his dedication, and at times his frustrating need for logical solutions to problems, SME might still be an idea whose time had not come. What started as David's summer job developed into a career as an SME member broker and option underwriter. The industry, like me, will be forever indebted to his unrelenting persistence.

David R. Capasso

Contents

Preface   **vii**
Acknowledgments   **xvii**

Chapter 1 **Building the Seattle Mercantile**
              Exchange   **1**

              Why the Seattle Mercantile Exchange
                 Was Organized   3
              The Beginning of SME   11
              Exchange-Traded Options   24
              Commodities (Genera) Traded and
                 Their Related Codes   26
              Market Size   26

Chapter 2 **The Origins of Futures Contracts,**
              Forward Contracts, and Option
              Contracts   **29**

              The Progression of Futures Trading   31
              Development of the Futures Contract   34

Chapter 3   **SME Trading Structure and Exercise Procedures**   **39**

Computerized Trading at SME   41

Guaranteed Contract Performance   43

Types of Options   48

American and European Styles
of Options   52

The Option Contract   53

Chapter 4   **Cash Market Issues**   **65**

The Local Cash Market   67

Local Market Alternatives   68

Various Cash Market Alternatives   68

Chapter 5   **Basis Makes Up the Difference**   **73**

What Is Basis?   75

Calculating Basis   75

Location and Basis   77

Passage of Time and Basis   78

Local Cash Prices and Distant
Forward Contract Months   79

The Importance of Local Basis   79

Basis Records   80

Basis Charts   80

Basis Predicted   81

Basis and Cash Prices   82

Chapter 6   **Forward Market Hedging**   **85**

Hedging and Its Purpose   87

Lifting a Hedge   89

Growers, Basis, and Hedging: What
Is the Best Delivery Month?   90
A Market for Speculating   92

Chapter 7   Marketing and Pricing   93

Forward Market Performance   95
Forward Price Determination   95
Forward Price Analysis   95
Forward Contract Prices and
Future Delivery   100
Location Can Affect Returns   101

Chapter 8   Forecasting Forward Prices   105

Introduction to Forecasting
Forward Prices   107
Forward Contract Pricing   107
The Fundamental No-Arbitrage
Equation   108
Convenience Value   111
Transformable Commodities   117

Chapter 9   Primary Option Pricing   125

How the Option Premium Is Set   127
Option Pricing and Forward Contracts   129
Intrinsic Value and Time Value   133
Pricing Summary   136
Case Study: Option Premium
Determination   136
Other Pricing Factors   140
Option Pricing Models   140
Black and Scholes's Formula   145

CONTENTS

Chapter 10 **Inventory, Hedging, and Speculating Strategies** **149**

Buying Calls   151
Selling Calls   155
Uncovered Call Writing   159
Buying Put Options   160
Selling Put Options   164
Covered Put Writing   165
Uncovered Put Writing   165

Conclusion   **167**

Seattle Mercantile Exchange Quick Reference Guide for Risk Mangement   **171**

Glossary   **181**

Appendix   **195**

Index   **201**

1

Building the Seattle
Mercantile Exchange

WHY THE SEATTLE MERCANTILE
EXCHANGE WAS ORGANIZED

Before delving into the why and how of the Seattle Mercantile Exchange (SME), I want to share two beliefs that have guided my business career. The first, quoted by an early business mentor, is as follows:

> A business does not go out of business because of a lack of cash, but because of a lack of creativity.

The quotation may be considered simplistic; the meaning, however, is clear. Throwing money at a problem does not necessarily solve it. A bad business plan, no matter how well capitalized, is still just that.

The second belief is self-penned:

> If you do not comprehend the magnitude of the problem, you will never appreciate the value of the solution.

SME was organized specifically to solve a problem facing the nursery industry: the marketing and pricing inefficiency associated with the buying and selling of nursery stock. This book explores solutions that will further the industry's development and growth. In the tradition of commodity exchanges serving other agrarian industries, SME offers a centralized market in which options and forward contracts on various genera are traded. For the first time in the history of the nursery industry, a method for "competitive distribution and price discovery," by which all segments of the industry have equal access, has been organized.

The current cash market for the purchase, a sale, and distribution of nursery stock does serve a purpose; unfortunately, however, it is inefficient and does not have the best interests of two important industry segments—the grower and the end consumer—in mind. Currently, for reasons explained later in this chapter, nursery stock pricing at the grower level is heavily influenced by the distribution segment (resellers) of the industry. Growers are being paid as little as possible for their efforts, while consumers are paying as much as is possible for those efforts. For example, since 1984, prices from the grower to the wholesaler have increased marginally, by approximately 7%, whereas wholesale prices on that same inventory increased drastically, by nearly 50%. Unfortunately, growers are not benefiting from what end consumers are willing to pay for nursery stock.

The primary reason for the price increase discrepancy between the grower and wholesale level can be attributed to the overall inefficiency that exists within the wholesale distribution segment and throughout the industry's distribution system. Price increases by the wholesale segment, or demands to the grower for lower prices, have been necessary to mask problems associated with this inefficiency. Problems such as poor on-site inventory cost containment, lack of capital for maximizing inventory purchasing, and poor marketing and collection practices are a few examples that contribute to the increasing cost of doing business.

As the cost of doing business increases, so does the level of risk. To manage that risk, the distribution system has limited alternatives, forcing it either to seek lower prices from growers or higher prices from the end consumers. Unfortunately, for competitive reasons, growers cannot increase prices at the same rate as wholesalers to assist with their cost of doing business. The best they can do is to reduce costs. But as most persons who are in business know, there is a limit to cost reduction. The outcome—large and small growers still struggle year after year and elect to, or are forced to (in record numbers), go out of business.

In addition, as a means to manage their own inventory risk, landscape brokers and wholesalers are compounding the problem by seeking the right to cancel or scale back orders as a condition to purchase from growers. In essence, the brokers' and wholesalers' inventory risks are being managed at the growers' expense. This certainly serves the buyers' financial interests; however, since growers carry the load, they are being most affected.

Unfortunately, rather than lose a buyer, growers are in the unenviable position of having to accept these cancellation conditions. A conversation with a large broker confirmed this cash market risk-shifting approach. In rationalizing this tact, the broker believed that given they maintained contact with the growers, canceling or scaling back orders had little effect on the growers' business. Growers produce and write orders in anticipation of shipment; a telephone call to cancel an order only forces growers into finding new, last-minute buyers.

Moreover, this particular broker viewed SME as a potential competitor for sales, rather than as a vehicle to improve nursery stock buying. However, SME has many brokers active in the market that do not share the same view. The fact is, SME competition will not be from sales, as this broker believed, but from supply. Given that growers have no true, risk-shifting outlet as do buyers, the forward market can offer that outlet as well as other financial advantages not present on the cash market.

It goes without saying that increasing numbers of growers, both large and small, are assigning product to the forward market. Most of this product is last-minute "canceled order" inventory. Soon, however, as the growers become more educated with the forward market and their comfort level increases, they will be assigning a larger percentage of their inventory. It will only be a matter of time before the forward market, at least on the genus SME trades, *becomes* the market. Growers can no longer continue to shoulder the risk exclusively.

Certainly, these problems are not exclusive to the nursery industry. Most businesses operating in industries dominated by a distribution system experience the same inefficiencies. Most industries, however, are seeking solutions for the advancement of the entire industry; for example, increasingly more retail- and product-oriented companies are electing to sell directly to retail outlets. This has eliminated the need for these companies to rely on wholesalers to serve certain price sensitive accounts.

Interestingly, many wholesale operations are welcoming this developing distribution trend. Wholesalers are finding that this allows them to concentrate on smaller, specialized retailers who are not as price sensitive as larger retailers. Although the wholesalers' sales volume is decreasing, the margins on those sales are increasing. More emphasis can be placed on service that, in the final analysis, builds customer loyalty.

Now, before the wholesalers who are reading this book run to the bookstore demanding their money back, I am *not* suggesting the industry eliminate wholesalers. What I am suggesting is that wholesalers, to manage their risk better, must reconsider their operational structure and the methods by which they conduct business. To combat the risk, many wholesalers are beginning to be growers themselves. Although this is certainly an option, it is really only shifting the risk from one business area to another.

The main purpose of the wholesaler is to offer sales representation to growers, both large and small. With the advent of the nursery superstore or with more space being dedicated to nursery stock by nontraditional nursery stock retailers, however, many growers—encouraged by the retailer—are beginning to sell directly to the retailer. This situation where wholesalers, because of operational inefficiency and a redirection of their resources, have missed an opportunity. Grower-to-retailer sales will continue and is the fastest-growing segment of a grower's sales. Granted, the larger retailers are buying price. But they have determined that the risk (cost) associated with carrying the inventory, hiring buyers to seek out growers, supplying extra floor and inventory space, and so forth outweigh the cost associated with buying from a wholesaler.

You might think that this is a simplistic answer, and it is. The larger retailer, however, has figured it out and is willing to carry the risk. This is an example of risk shifting. Moreover, growers pursuing retailers are obviously willing to risk alienating wholesalers.

A study conducted by the Oregon Association of Nurserymen (OAN) demonstrated that Oregon growers shipped nearly $371 million in nursery stock in 1992. Of the approximately 1,700 growers surveyed, fewer than 200 represented $241 million of the total shipped. Clearly, those growers are better managed (i.e., have better production and marketing techniques) than the others and, therefore, can offer competitively priced, quality products. This situation has developed mostly to satisfy the needs of the superstores, which in some cases now represent 30% to 40% of the growers' business. But even the largest growers are currently feeling the effects of the wholesale segments needed to receive further price discounts on the 50% to 60% of the product not sold directly to retailers.

Unfortunately, due to poorly run operations, and a lack of capital and marketing practices, the smaller grower cannot compete with the larger growers. SME staff, during its field research, repeatedly heard how the smaller growers believed that the larger growers, to move product, were intentionally pricing product at or below cost. This, in turn, according to the smaller grower, caused them to lose market share. Moreover, the smaller growers believed that a bad precedent was being set; that is, as the national demand for nursery stock improves, which it will, buyers would continue to expect lower pricing. Needless to say, a tremendous amount of animosity was directed toward the larger growers.

Contrary to what many smaller growers want to believe, however, the larger grower does not care what the smaller grower is doing. If there is "dumping," it is used primarily to free space to develop new products or as loss leaders for developing future sales outlets, not to put smaller growers out of business. In fact, the larger growers, feeling the effect of demands for lower prices, have become far more efficient in developing products, and their pricing reflects that. Aggressive, ongoing price discounting is done for competitive reasons by and among larger growers. Unfortunately, as these entities fight for market share, smaller growers get caught in the middle. As price becomes the main competitive issue, it contributes to a feeding frenzy by the distribution segment; therein lies the problem.

In addition to the situations just outlined, Oregon growers (and all Northwest growers, for that matter) are affected by Eastern growers who are beginning to develop and sell nursery stock, an area dominated by Northwest growers for years. With 70% of the nursery stock grown in the Northwest being shipped east (a primary, lucrative market for Northwest growers), Northwest growers, to maintain their eastern market share and to ensure survival, are succumbing to further distribution segment demands, such as lower prices, liberal credit terms, and the right to cancel or scale back orders without recourse.

Given that wholesalers have yet to solve their internal business and operating problems, they are left with no other alternatives but to raise wholesale prices, to seek lower prices, or to cancel orders. A simple analogy is the workings of government. Rather than improve the operation of government to reduce costs, it is sometimes easier to raise taxes.

Needless to say, the nursery industry is changing—many say for the better—but at what cost? Growers going out of business for whatever reasons benefit no one. Thus demanding lower prices to mask distribution inefficiency is clearly not the answer.

Because of the risk associated with cash market transactions, the industry has developed and implemented creative solutions to overcome this inherent risk. To operate successfully within the system, risk shifting is accomplished by maintaining flexibility (wheeling and dealing on price and supply), while being careful to stay within the guidelines of ethical practices. It is not uncommon for the industry to short material to clients or to ship inferior material as a means of dumping risk.

Simply stated, a noncommittal approach to buying or selling, while always seeking better last-minute deals, is the industry's answer to cash market risk shifting. This wheeling and dealing approach, however, creates mistrust within all industry segments and, without question, is inefficient and costly.

One approach that supports the industry's need for flexibility is option use, which allows segments to secure quality material for future use with minimal capital outlay (leverage, the ultimate price and supply hedge). By incorporating option trading into their business planning, the industry can satisfy supply, inventory, and pricing obstacles. Moreover, options offer the industry an opportunity to wheel and deal far more effectively— at less cost and risk and without unnecessary wear and tear and unethical practices. In addition, by allowing all industry segments equal access to the market, fair market price discovery is accomplished.

Forward markets, which SME offers, address the inefficiency inherent in a cash market. This is accomplished by allowing all industry segments an opportunity for efficient price discovery and for shifting risk associated with the growing, selling, and buying of nursery stock. SME offers an efficient, competitive price-discovery mechanism that allows prices to respond immediately to changing supply and demand. The SME forward market provides a "risk-sharing" function for growers, landscape brokers, wholesalers, garden centers, and so on by allowing price and inventory risk to be spread equally throughout the industry.

As this book thoroughly explains, this shifting of risk equally throughout the various industry segments improves trade efficiency. The forward market, unlike the cash market, advances the market's financial stability by offering risk-shifting opportunities and price cohesiveness.

Historically, the industry's only recourse to manage risk adversity, inherent in a cash market, has been to seek lower prices from the grower or higher prices from the end user. Those solutions do little to strengthen the industry's financial structure and, in fact, work contrary to the market's efficiency.

The long-term effect derived from a forward market is an efficient market for the benefit of all industry segments. The industry is financially too large to continue to be served exclusively by the cash market. With fewer banks financing grower and buyer inventories, the industry's already tight capital must be used efficiently. The forward market supports the effective use of that capital.

Both growers and nursery material buyers, such as landscape contractors, wholesalers, and retailers, need efficient forward pricing to anticipate costs and to operate profitably. If a reduction in price-level risk was possible, it would lower the cost of doing business. Price-level changes caused by fluctuations in areas such as consumer demand, over- or undersupply of material, and availability or cost of capital can mean the difference between financial profit or loss. The ability to trade options on forward contracts offers the industry a marketing, financing, and risk management alternative to the regressive cash market, at least on the genus SME trades.

THE BEGINNING OF SME

The Initial Idea

I moved to Seattle, Washington, in the summer of 1991, to complete an 8-week consulting assignment unrelated to the nursery industry. I was planning to leave for San Diego in September to complete a business book that I had started writing the previous year. Seattle was an interesting place—the people, the area, and the summer climate were delightful. It was certainly better than the humid summer climate I was accustomed to growing up in Connecticut. For various business reasons, I decided to stay in Seattle until June 1992.

Three years earlier, I had sold my publishing company, which I had founded in 1979. This company published trade magazines and books for small businesses. I had written many of the books that we published. Needless to say, as a result, I had first-hand experience with marketing, finance, staff, and, of course, banks.

The idea for SME came about when I accompanied a colleague, a Seattle-based landscape contractor, on a tree-buying trip to Oregon in March 1992. He was attempting to purchase nearly $1 million of highly specialized, sculptured pines. The grower, after 10 years of development, was in the market introduction stage of his trees. My colleague was attempting to secure (from the grower) the exclusive rights to sell the trees in the Seattle and Vancouver, British Columbia, markets. Because banks were not taking an aggressive role in the financing of nursery inventory and my colleague was cash deficient, he needed a creative financing solution to obtain the inventory and related marketing rights. Armed with what he believed to be a comprehensive business and marketing plan, he set out to secure the grower's inventory.

During the 3-hour drive from Seattle to Portland, he asked me to review his business plan. Although colorful and detailed, the business plan was absent one critical element: money. The business plan asked for marketing exclusives but offered few guarantees that the grower would ever receive orders. Although well intended (and if successful, beneficial to the grower), the plan lacked a motivational element for the grower to accept what basically was an inventory consignment arrangement. This arrangement, in the early stages of the plan's implementation, would exclusively benefit my colleague.

With experience in creative finance and related business matters, I suggested the following: for the grower to accept the business plan, my colleague should offer the grower "deposit" money. If the marketing plan failed and orders were not forthcoming, the grower could keep the deposit. I referred to the deposit as "option" money, or a fraction of the total price of the inventory my colleague sought to secure.

Certainly, the use of deposit money is not new to the nursery industry. Deposits on future delivery are the backbone of the business. The idea of option money for the intended purpose of giving the buyer the right, but not the obligation, to purchase inventory, however, is not used by the nursery industry with any regularity. With deposits, growers feel somewhat secure that they have sales, and purchase orders are written in anticipation of delivery and final payment. Regardless of deposits, growers rarely enter into purchase orders that are planned for cancellation. The idea of fronting option money to obtain a contract from the grower with a built-in cancellation clause and 3 years of guaranteed inventory prices was certainly new. Moreover, it was an idea that might be difficult, at best, to sell to the grower.

I also suggested to my colleague that because he was planning to sell the trees to the trade—wholesalers, garden centers, landscape contractors, and so on—and not to the end consumer, offering the same rights to those interested in buying the trees as were given to the grower for selling might make selling the trees easier. There were many advantages to this approach. The grower wanted to sell and the buyer wanted to buy, so all that was needed to accomplish this objective was an amicable arrangement that went beyond the traditional deposit/purchase order method. We needed something more creative.

Many persons believe a business plan should focus on the company's or product's profit potential. I have on many occasions read dissertations, pounds of pulp, dedicated to how much money the investors or principals could earn. As someone who has written quite a few business plans, as well as several books on the subject, I have had first-hand experience with the makings of a successful business plan.

Readers of business plans inevitably are concerned with one issue, and one issue only, risk. How much and for how long? Granted, money motivates, but by and large, investors (especially bankers) are motivated by keeping what they already have. Therefore, a successful business plan must consider, first and foremost, the risk to those financing the business plan or, in this case, the trees. For a business plan to be considered, the risk associated must be a thread woven throughout the plan that will hold the plan together.

I remember one business plan written for the purpose of a business owner seeking money for his company's expansion. After it was read by the investor, the two met to discuss the possibility of any future business dealings. The investor, however, was rightfully concerned about his risk and began questioning the owner. After many pointed questions, the owner spoke up:

"Wait a minute," he offered, "I realize you're concerned about your money, but I have a fortune invested here, your loss is my loss."

The investor, leaning forward, looked into the owner's eyes and stated, "You obviously have mistaken me for someone who cares about your risk."

I thanked the man for his time, revised my plan, and returned a week later to learn we had a deal.

Aside from highlighting risk and the means to avoid it, my experience suggests that a business plan should offer the reader a unique perspective on the featured company or product. One that even the reader has not considered. Without question, math and logic need to make sense, but as important as these elements are, the business plan also needs a spirit—a sense that, regardless of what fate brings, those involved are committed to the plan's outcome. The plan also should make financial and economic sense, as well as contain an emotional element.

I suggested that my colleague forgo his scheduled presentation with the grower until the next day, while I developed a new business plan based on an option program to secure the inventory. My argument to my colleague was that if the grower does not accept the plan, most likely, there may not be another opportunity to resubmit a new, no money down, plan. Fortunately, he agreed.

To better understand the product for which I was to write a plan, I asked my colleague for a tour of the grower's operation. Writers, even business plan writers, need inspiration. Merely reducing numbers to a page does not necessarily make a successful business plan. The reader of a business plan will understand numbers, particularly when the numbers pertain to their operation.

My colleague did not fully grasp why I wanted to walk through a tree farm at 6:00 A.M., but he begrudgingly arranged for the visit.

"What are you expecting to see . . . deer frolicking, snow-capped mountains, rolling hills?" he asked jokingly.

"Yes," I replied.

"We're not going to Yellowstone. It's a tree farm," he quipped.

As we drove down the long driveway to the farm, I could see thousands of trees lining the hillside. As I walked the alleys, trees were everywhere. Neatly planted were row after row of trees almost as far as I could see. No, I did not see deer frolicking or snow-capped mountains. As the sun was rising, however, I saw the most beautiful landscape in the country. High on a hill overlooking a valley, I stood witness to one person's hard work and dedication. Even I, with no experience in the nursery industry, could appreciate the grower who had painstakingly planted, nurtured, and with a tremendous love for his work built what I was about to reduce to writing. I was overwhelmed by the sheer beauty of the land.

How was I to capture in mere words what was obviously in the grower's heart? How was I to convince him that we understood his years of hard work and sacrifice and that, if given the opportunity, my colleague could sell more trees in a shorter period of time then he, the grower, could do on his own? Indeed, this was to be a challenging task.

As I worked my way down the hill, I knew that I wanted to be involved with this project. It was as if someone, without saying it aloud, had said to me, "This is the business you should be in." At the time, I had no idea of what that business was. In fact, I was in no hurry to get back into business. After 10 years of building a company, the motivation to do it again was not there. I was content, at least for a few more years, with writing, consulting, and traveling.

While I was growing up, a friend of mine, the least likely person that you could imagine, was planning to become a priest. The Bowery Boys of East Side Gang fame were saints compared to this lad. Although mischievous, he was certainly religious.

> I remember asking him, "Why a priest? How do you know that's what life has to offer you?"
>
> "Simply," he replied, "it was a calling. I was in Church one day . . . I knew it was where I belonged. As if someone said, without saying it, you're home."

Until that day in March 1992, nearly 20 years after my friend told me of his calling, I did not understand what he had meant. Other than the goal of creating a business plan that satisfied the needs of the grower and my colleague, I had no idea of what was ahead for me.

That afternoon, a presentation was made to the grower based on the new option plan. The process of developing an option program to secure inventory had begun. My colleague asked the grower for and was granted 90 days to develop the option plan further. In turn, I was commissioned to advance the economics of my option theory.

Interestingly, my colleague had little confidence that the grower would accept the option concept. "This industry," he expounded, "is unlike any other industry that you have worked in or written for. It accepts new ideas and change with absolute reluctance." Therefore, he viewed the 90-day period as an opportunity to find the money to secure the inventory. His confidence in my ability was not a priority to him.

From the beginning, my plan was not to build an exchange for the nursery industry. My work to develop an options program that was acceptable to the grower and to my colleague's financial situation and to help to sell trees led to one conclusion. *If option contracts could satisfy their*

16

particular buy/sell dilemma, a centralized market for the trading of options might serve the needs of others within the nursery industry. This thought was confirmed when I began researching options and their underlying forward contracts. With little knowledge of commodity exchanges, I set out to understand the mechanics and advantages of exchange trading.

The Research

My first journey was to the grandfather of commodity exchanges, the Chicago Board of Trade (CBOT), founded in 1848. After weeks of classes, I returned to Seattle with a list of recommended reading (nearly 50 books on the subject of exchange trading). After a year of what seemed to be 7-day work weeks, I developed the structure of a commodity exchange for trading contracts on select nursery stock.

I concluded that although exchanges assisted with marketing an industry's product and solved many operational questions, an exchange's purpose went beyond efficient selling procedures. Its purpose was to manage risk, particularly risk associated with cash market transactions. As time progressed, I learned more about the nursery industry's cash market and began to realize that risk permeated the industry. The only ways the industry sought to manage that risk was to seek lower prices from the grower or higher prices from the consumer.

Not only had I stumbled onto improving marketing and pricing procedures, I had opened the door to the industry's biggest problem: How do we shift risk effectively and equally throughout the industry? (Chapter 2 looks at the evolution of the forward market.) It is important to note, however, that a forward market does not replace a cash market. It works in conjunction with the cash market. The forward market is used to offset the risk in one's cash market positions. It is not the end result, but merely a tool, albeit an efficient tool.

Throughout the year, I informed the grower and my colleague of my progress. At the time, the grower employed a vice-president in charge of operations who was knowledgeable about exchange trading and the purpose of exchanges. He was intrigued with the idea of a commodity exchange operating within the nursery industry. Accordingly, pending my final presentation, the vice-president kept the option idea alive with the grower. Over the 18-month development period I had visited the fields numerous times, mostly alone, often wondering if selling trees was what I was supposed to be doing at this point in my business career.

Once the exchange structure was formulated, work began on the regulatory front. It was assumed that if the exchange operated solely for the benefit of the nursery industry and if the public was not allowed to trade, exemptions from the numerous regulations that govern exchange trading may exist. The Commodity Futures Trading Commission (CFTC), like the Securities and Exchange Commission (SEC) that oversees the securities business, is empowered to protect the interests of the public by ensuring that futures contracts traded on commodity exchanges are consistent and that the market for which the contracts served was stable. In months of research I discovered that there were exemptions for "trade options," which are options used to facilitate commerce (trade) within an industry.

After months of correspondence and numerous telephone conversations with CFTC attorneys in Washington, DC, the CFTC, in a verbal opinion, "found no reason why SME trade options were not exempt." In other words, as long as SME trading is done by those involved commercially with the industry, the option and forward contracts being offered are exempt from CFTC regulations.

With exemption in hand, I began to develop a national SME member broker network and to secure growers to participate in the forward market. There are now 25 independently owned brokerage firms, members of SME, operating throughout the United States with a total of 50 planned for mid-1995 (see appendix for complete list). In addition, SME has reached its first-year inventory goal committed to the forward market.

Eighteen months from the time I conceived and introduced my colleague's grower to the option idea, the grower became the first to participate, committing nearly $4 million of inventory to the forward market. By then, without any prospect of ever trading an option, I had spent, or committed obligations to spend, nearly $250,000 in development cost. This did not include the cost to launch, fund marketing, and operations. Even though all new ventures have start-up costs, the idea of an exchange for an industry that was conservative in its thinking and that approached change reluctantly was a risky venture, to say the least.

Fortunately, my resources were such that I did not have to visit my old friend, now retired, with a business plan in search of cash to build the exchange. I did, however, confer with him about the direction I should take.

"Always remember the risk," he stated.

"Mine?" I questioned.

"No, the industry's," he said adamantly. "Don't confuse them with people who care about your risk."

That statement had once again served to remind me of an important fact: Understand and explain the risk.

By December 1993, after 2 years of development work, I had devised the plan for the Seattle Mercantile Exchange. Never before had I become so consumed as I was when developing the exchange. My mind was constantly focused on the plan. Given that an exchange had never operated within the nursery industry, I had to raise and answer my own questions. Needless to say, I often found myself arguing with myself in public places.

In fact, my obsession with building the exchange was so perverse that if a restaurant had cloth napkins, I would panic—I would have nowhere to jot my notes. Interestingly, I found that walking helped. I sold my car and began using public transportation. This forced me to take time away from my work and gave me more time to think, write, and argue. Fortunately, my lady friend lived on the bus route, although she never could understand or appreciate my penchant for riding the bus.

Implementing SME

On May 6, 1993, the exchange was incorporated, and months of continued research and test trading began. The exchange officially opened for business in January 1994, almost 2 years from the day I first walked through a tree farm, in March 1992. After a 5-year sabbatical, I was back to running a company. My role was now to work with the nursery industry on education, public relations, and marketing.

On Christmas day 1993, after almost 2 years of living and working on this project in Seattle, I boarded a plane for Connecticut. Although I was planning to spend only a week or so visiting friends and family for the holidays, I decided it was time to take a long overdue and deserved rest. I secured a wonderful home on the Connecticut shore, along a 1-mile stretch of mostly summer homes. I went from a city apartment overlooking shipping commerce in Puget Sound to birds on Long Island Sound.

My development work completed, it was now time to contemplate the future of the Seattle Mercantile Exchange, its relationship within the nursery industry, and my relationship with it. It was also time to make the mental transition from development to implementation.

The first month, January 1994, I spent talking to the birds, trying my best to keep warm. It seems that I had picked one of the coldest and snowiest winters on record to return. By February, I was discussing SME with the

Wall Street types. Every other day I was on the train from Connecticut to New York City. One person in particular, Tom Walker, was extremely helpful. I had met him on one of my many research trips back east and had immediately respected his knowledge on exchange structure and purpose. He had long been involved with commodity exchanges, and as a trader, educator, and exchange executive, he knew the business of an exchange. I had supplied him with my work, and although he did not know the dynamics of the nursery industry, he knew an exchange when he saw one. His approval was important, not to the nursery industry or the financial community, but to me, and it showed for the first time in 2 years that my work was sound.

Tom offered one very important bit of advice. As we stood in the observation deck overlooking the trading floor of the New York Merc, Cotton Exchange, COMEX, sugar, coffee, and cocoa exchanges, all housed under one roof at New York's World Trade Center, he said, "Informing the industry about the exchange is one thing, getting them to use it is another. Educating the market is paramount." As I watched with utter amazement, as most first-time observers do, the hands, arms, and fingers of these traders were frantically flying. I wondered how I was going to explain this back in Oregon. As Albert Pacelli describes it:

> There, on the exchange floor, 50 or 60 grown men stood leaning in each other's faces shouting as loudly as they could in primordial tones of voice that I had never heard before, except maybe the one time I tried to take a shrimp away from my cat, Paco. Veins bulged in the men's necks. Their eyes seemed ready to leap from their sockets at any moment. They waved their arms threateningly at one another in some incomprehensible code.
>
> It was like a cockfight without the cocks. A crowd this angry couldn't help but come to blows at any

moment. . . . My heart was in my throat. What was going on here?

The men were trading cotton.*

In March 1994, I completed this book. I can appreciate the anxiety of those that have built careers in academia and then, for whatever reason, are thrust into the outside world to earn a living. I once heard someone say, when comparing the business world to academics, "In business it's dog eat dog, in academia, it's visa versa." For me, the 2 years of theory and paper napkins, my academia, were over. It was now time to educate the industry and to build a forward market.

This book is a business plan that instructs how to use the exchange to manage the risk, how to improve marketing, and how to solve operational questions associated with the buying and selling of certain nursery stock on the cash market. This business plan, and the foundation on which SME was built, considers risk, the thread that holds the book together.

As stated, the purpose of an exchange (a forward market) is to spread risk equally throughout the industry. The cash market is fraught with risk. I have tried to demonstrate to the industry that risk can be managed, certainly better than the current cash market. This work offers testimony to that accomplishment.

Genera Selection

Many thoughts about the criteria used for selecting the genera and species to be traded and the type of contracts to offer were discussed. Two key concerns for genera selection were (1) genera with a history of price volatility and annual supply uncertainty and (2) a market demand and long-term supply projections. A year of research and interviews

---

*Albert Pacelli, as quoted in *Option Market Making* by Allen Jan Baird, 1991, New York: John Wiley & Sons.

with various industry segments produced the following genera: *Acer, Cercidiphyllum, Fagus, Liquidambar, Picea,* and *Pinus.*

Trees were selected because they demonstrated far greater price and supply volatility than other plant genera. SME research suggested that the genera selected for trading, in contrast to other tree genera, are the most popular and satisfy a larger geographic area of the U.S. market (growers and survival climate) and historically are the most price and supply volatile of all tree genera.

In addition, it is better to be an expert and to be recognized in *one* category, thereby developing for the exchange what is commonly known in consumer marketing as "brand recognition." Most, if not all, commodity exchanges specialize in a limited number of commodities for the particular industry they serve. For example, the Minneapolis Grain Exchange was built on trading spring red wheat contracts. Similarly, the New York coffee, cocoa, and sugar exchanges and the New York Cotton Exchange handle specific commodities. Seattle Mercantile Exchange shall become the exchange for select genera that demonstrate the described criteria. Additions or deletions to the list will be governed by market demand and long-term supply.

The SME Today

Currently, SME conducts seminars to educate the industry on the use of options and forward contracts to secure inventory, for both hedging and speculation purposes. The nursery industry is certainly large enough to offer the liquidity necessary to develop an orderly, efficient forward market. SME's short-term goal is to educate and introduce as many buyers and sellers to the forward market to support liquidity expansion as possible.

SME's long-term quest is to develop an "institution" that serves the economic interests of those commercially engaged in the nursery industry; and, I remain committed to that proposition. Only the industry will decide if it needs a forward market. It is my conviction, and that of others who are both within the nursery industry and who have made a career working with exchanges, that it does. If the industry takes the time to learn and understand how a forward market works, then it will come to the same, obvious conclusion.

EXCHANGE-TRADED OPTIONS

Options are financial instruments that can provide nursery professionals with the flexibility needed in almost any speculation or hedge situation encountered. Options give you options. You are not just limited to buying, selling, or staying out of the market. With options, you can tailor your inventory requirements or hedging position to suit your own needs. For example, consider the following potential benefits of options. They

- Protect against a decline in nursery inventory price.
- Increase income against current holdings.
- Prepare you to buy inventory at a lower price.
- Provide you with a benefit from a nursery inventory price rise or fall.

The Forward Market

The nursery materials forward market is where financial instruments (contracts) for the future delivery of nursery material are bought and sold. These instruments include items as forward contracts, which arrange for delivery at a later date at a set price, or options on forward contracts, which give the holder the right (but not the obligation) to purchase a forward contract before a specified date.

The term *markets* refers to the buyers of the contracts, which can include growers, landscape brokers, wholesalers, rewholesalers, landscape contractors, landscape architects, retail garden centers, and all those needing to purchase nursery inventory. Trading, however, is limited to those commercially involved with the nursery industry.

Benefits of Exchange-Traded Options

The major benefits of option trading are: orderly, efficient, and liquid markets; guaranteed contract performance; flexibility; leverage; and limited risk. Because of a high degree of contract standardization, a secondary market exists. Both options and forward contracts can be bought and sold (traded), prior to expiration date, on this secondary market. This presence of a secondary market allows for optimum financial planning and liquidity. Options offer a short-term (months) as well as a long-term (up to 3 years) hedge. Whether you seek a short- or long-term hedge, options can assist with almost any strategy.

Example: A landscape architect owns an option to purchase a forward contract. If she discovers that there is no longer a need for this material, she can sell the option on the secondary market to a landscape contractor or other industry professional.

The interactions of nursery professionals define the nursery materials forward market. Seattle Mercantile Exchange oversees the original issuing of the contracts and processes and clears all subsequent trades. Simply stated, the exchange offers buyers and sellers the ability to hedge against price and to secure inventory for future delivery.

Despite the many benefits of forward contract options, individuals should not enter into option transactions until they have read and understood all exchange documentation. Such documentation can be obtained from an SME member broker or from the exchange directly. The intent of this book is to offer the reader a working knowledge of forward contract options and their use; the exchange and member brokers can supply the rules and regulations regarding trading and settlement procedures.

As with any commodity or stock exchange, under certain conditions it may be difficult or impossible to liquidate an option position when desired, despite the efforts of Seattle Mercantile Exchange to provide liquid markets. Literature supplied by member brokers further discusses this issue. In addition, transaction and commission costs and tax ramifications of buying or selling options should be discussed thoroughly with a broker or tax adviser before engaging in option transactions.

COMMODITIES (GENERA) TRADED AND THEIR RELATED CODES

The commodity code is generated by piecing together the ticker symbol, the material's root form, and the appropriate size code (see Table 1.1).

MARKET SIZE

A U.S. Department of Commerce census study demonstrates that national sales of landscape material (nursery/greenhouse stock) has increased from $3.2 billion annually in 1982 to an estimated $6 billion in 1992. The figures equate to nearly $15 billion on the consumer level. A U.S. landscape tree-planting survey released May 22, 1992, sponsored by the American Association of Nurserymen (AAN) and the USDA Forest Service, suggests that from October 1, 1990, to September 30, 1991, 105,636,000 trees (used in landscape design) were grown and sold in the United States (see Table 1.2). The survey suggests that 1993/1994 landscape tree production may increase 29% above the 1990/1991 level, from 105,635,000 to 135,790,000.

TABLE 1.1
TICKER SYMBOLS AND COMMODITY CODES

Ticker Symbol	Botanical Name	Common Name
ACRPL	*Acer palmatum*	Japanese maple
ACRPLAT	*Acer palmatum atropurpureum*	Red Japanese maple
ACRPLDS	*Acer palmatum dissectum*	Japanese L.L. maple
CRCJP	*Cercidiphyllum japonicum*	Katsura tree
FGSSL	*Fagus sylvatica*	European beech
FGSSLRV	*Fagus sylvatica riversi*	River's purple beech
LQDST	*Liquidamba styraciflua*	American sweetgum
PCAPN	*Picea pungens*	Colorado spruce
PCAPNGL	*Picea pungens glauca*	Colorado blue spruce
PNSNG	*Pinus nigra*	Austrian black pine
PNSSL	*Pinus sylvatica*	Scotch pine
PNSTH	*Pinus thunbergii*	Black pine

Root Code	Root Form	Size Code	Size
1	Balled and burlapped	C100	Caliper 1"
2	Container	C125	Caliper 1.25"
3	Grow bag	C150	Caliper 1.5"
4	Processed ball	C175	Caliper 1.75"
5	Bare root	C200	Caliper 2"
6	Pot	C250	Caliper 2.5"
7	Hanging basket	C300	Caliper 3"
8	Box	C350	Caliper 3.5"
9	Basket	C400	Caliper 4"
0	Other	H048	Height 4'
		H060	Height 5'
		H072	Height 6'
		H084	Height 7'
		H096	Height 8'
		H108	Height 9'
		H120	Height 10'
		H132	Height 11'
		H144	Height 12'

TABLE 1.2
TREES USED IN LANDSCAPE DESIGN,
OCT. 1, 1990–SEPT. 30, 1991

Type of Tree	Trees Sold
Deciduous shade trees	33,073,000
Deciduous flowering trees	25,297,000
Broadleaf and/or coniferous evergreen trees	39,175,000
Fruit and/or nut trees	8,091,000
Total	105,636,000

Distribution Channel	Trees Sold
Garden centers	35,916,000
Landscape contractors	23,240,000
Rewholesalers and horticultural distributors	21,127,000
Municipalities or governments	4,225,000
General merchandisers	16,902,000
Others	4,225,000
Total	105,635,000

Of the over 135 million trees, SME estimates that nearly 14 million are of the same genus and species as those offered for trade on the exchange in 1994, with an estimated value of $2 billion. The exchange plans to secure from growers throughout the country, and make available for trade, approximately 20% of that total, creating a $500 million forward market.

Therefore, the opinion of SME management, given the low percentage of trees that the exchange plans to offer for trade compared with the total purchased by the distribution channels outlined, is that the probability for market acceptance and the development of the secondary market for exchange-related contracts is extremely high.

The Origins of Futures Contracts, Forward Contracts, and Option Contracts

The history of options is believed to date back several centuries, but standardized, government-regulated, exchange-listed options were not available until 1973. In just a few years, these options became a necessary tool of the securities industry. Options on futures contracts, tools of trade for the commodity industry, are also comparatively new. Nonetheless, the history of trading standardized contracts was many centuries in the making.

THE PROGRESSION OF FUTURES TRADING

Trade many years ago transpired over great distances. The trade networks of the Phoenician, Greek, Roman, and Byzantine empires were primary sources of economic power for these civilizations. Given the hazards of travel, only trading on barter and cash-and-carry bases was conducted. With the decline of the Roman Empire, territories in Europe became disorganized and hostile. Quarrels between regions began to undermine the transfer of goods. With the demise of Rome's urban tradition, only a few cities in the south of France and Italy maintained ties with distant Far East trade markets. During the Middle Ages, economic and political stability slowly returned. In the eleventh and twelfth centuries, several warring monarchs succeeded in expanding their land holdings, which in turn became the modern European state system.

With a revival in trade during the twelfth century, two main trading centers developed on the European continent. In northern Italy the cities of Venice, Florence, Genoa, and Pisa sought to expand their trade throughout Europe. So did the northern European trade center of the Flanders region (now Holland and Belgium). Known for fine cloth, the Flanders region had strong economic ties to England, then the most important wool-producing region in Europe. Specializing in such luxuries as fine silk, spices, rare metals, and exotic perfumes, Italian traders, on land controlled by the Counts of Champagne, crossed paths with Flemish traders of cloth, wine, salt fish, lumber, and metalware. In 1114 the Counts of Champagne, to encourage trade activity (for which they received fees), established trade fairs. It was at these trade markets the first use of forward contracts occurred.

The market fairs became primary centers of exchange. Traders, not only from Flanders and Italy but from Scandinavia, England, and even Russia, participated. The Counts of Champagne provided protection, money changers, and even storage facilities. Trade fairs developed into year-round events, eventually specializing in select commodities; at Reims it was leather and skins, and at Troyes, linen and wool.

Typically, the last days of each fair were used for paying bills and settling accounts. Because traders came from throughout the region and from varied ethnic backgrounds, account settlement disputes were common. To avoid these disputes a code of commercial law, called the "law merchant," was developed. Violators of the code were taken before "courts of the fair," supervised by merchants, to argue their case and to seek settlement.

This mercantile law functioned much the same as the regulations established by today's exchanges. The mercantile law defined contract terms, established methods of sampling, inspecting, grading, and predetermined the location and date for the commodity's delivery. Although most transactions were spot market in nature, an innovation of the medieval fairs was a forward contract document called a *lettre de faire* (letter of the fair) that specified delivery at a later date. First issued only in the sale of cash commodities between a single buyer and seller, these *lettres de faire* evolved into standardized, negotiable documents that could be transferred to several parties before the commodity arrived at the warehouse for storage.

With travel difficult, many merchants preferred to bring only commodity samples to the fairs, and the *lettre de faire* made trade by sample acceptable to both the buyer and the seller. The function of a *lettre de faire* became similar to the bill of exchange in use today. A *lettre de faire* had characteristics of the modern warehouse receipt in that it was signed by a merchant in a far-off city and indicated that a specified commodity was being held in a warehouse. The receipt could be sold to a third party who could then either sell or take possession of the commodity. This forward contract trading in the late Middle Ages was similar to modern futures contracts; forward trades, however, were consummated on a personal basis and lacked standardization.

With the establishment of the Champagne market fairs and others like them at Bruges, Antwerp, and Amsterdam, and with the acceptance of trade by sample for certain commodity transactions, England created year-round meeting places known as exchanges. Here traders could buy and sell commodities. An early example is the royal exchange opened in London in 1570. This later divided into specialized exchanges known as the London Commodity Exchange.

In return for the opportunity to profit in forward transactions, middlemen, known as dealers, were willing to accept price risks that merchants wished to avoid. Cash trades remained the essential part of the market, but increasing numbers of traders were taking advantage of forward contracts. With the evolving system, sellers sold their merchandise to dealers, who in turn sought prospective buyers. Sellers with reasonable prices were sure to sell their wares, and on the other hand, buyers could receive standardized levels of quality from dealers. At this point in time, grading systems and futures contracts were not yet contrived, but they were not far off.

DEVELOPMENT OF THE FUTURES CONTRACT

The first case of organized futures trading occurred in Japan in the 1600s. In lieu of cash, wealthy landowners accepted a share of each year's rice harvest from tenants. But the money economy required landowners to have cash on hand. Income from harvests was irregular; the need for income stability stimulated the practice of shipping surplus rice to cities where it could be stored and sold when needed. In an effort to raise cash, landlords sold tickets (warehouse receipts) against rice stored in warehouses. Rice tickets were used as a form of currency to facilitate the transaction of business. Merchants generally bought these tickets in anticipation of their projected needs. Stored rice reserves, however, were often inadequate. When this occurred, merchants would extend credit to landlords, at interest, prior to the actual sale of the rice tickets.

During the late seventeenth century, futures contracts were the only form of trade permitted at the Japanese Dojima rice market. By 1730, the imperial government named and officially recognized the market as *cho-ai-mai*, or "rice trade on book." A number of rules of the marketplace were remarkably similar to today's American futures trading rules: Contract terms were of limited duration, contracts were standardized, contract periods were agreed on beforehand, contracts could not be carried into new contract periods, trades were cleared through, and traders had to establish lines of credit with the clearinghouse.

The *cho-ai-mai* market, unlike today's futures market, never permitted delivery of cash commodities. This "futures trading only" concept, however, caused the relationship between futures and cash prices to function improperly; consequently, erratic price fluctuations transpired.

Ultimately, the tying of the cash to the futures market in Japan was introduced, which may have been influenced by Western trading practices. During the early part of the nineteenth century, as the economy in the United States expanded, commodity exchanges evolved from unorganized club-type associations into formalized exchanges. The Chicago Board of Trade, established in 1848 with 82 members, was the first. Encouraged by the trading standards, inspection system, and weighing system prescribed by the board, the first time contract was traded on March 13, 1851.

Matching in nature a *lettre de faire*, forward contracts known as "to arrive" contracts appeared in the middle of the nineteenth century. Because of the increased volume of trading at Chicago, the risk in forward contracts became so great that transferring to agents or specialized dealers, common in the London markets, was not enough; if a third party could assume risk, the effect would be the same as using dealers, with an assurance of a quality product at a fair price for the seller.

The first "to arrive" contracts, however, were not transferable, but printed documents, developed to specify the grade, quantity, and the commodity's delivery time, were. Alterations to the "to arrive" contracts created the futures market in which a contract was easily tradable before delivery. The dealer or "speculator" in the newly evolving U.S. marketing structure is where risk was placed.

With the increasing volume of futures contracts trading in Chicago and the introduction of the speculator to replace the London-type dealer, additional rules for orderly and equitable futures trading were needed. Commodities had to be easily graded and be maintained by regular governmental inspection, and payment had to be set at the time of delivery. In addition, price discovery had to be open and equally accessible to all traders. Buyers and sellers were required to establish financial responsibility, and the number of sellers had to remain large enough to provide continuous opportunities, or liquidity.

Trading on the Chicago Board of Trade was considerable. By 1870, futures trading had begun on the New York Produce Exchange and the New York Cotton Exchange. By 1885, the New York Coffee Exchange was actively trading in futures. Since the second half of the nineteenth century, other commodity exchanges have been founded. In fact, the growth of this institution has been continuous since 1865. The U.S. commodity futures market has developed into approximately 10 major and minor exchanges.

Since the introduction of stock option trading in 1974 and futures (commodities) option trading in 1982, the total volume of option trading on all exchanges and over-the-counter markets in the United States is now billions of dollars a day. Option trading is one of the largest and most rapidly growing sectors of the financial industry. After a lag of about a decade, the options market of Europe and Asia are following the growth path of the United States, promising that world option markets will become one of the most important sectors of the global financial industry in the 1990s and probably into the next century.*

In 1974, when stock options were first introduced, approximately 1 million option contracts were traded. Today nearly 110 million contracts are traded annually. On the world's futures markets, nearly 300 million options were traded in 1993, representing an increase over 1992 of 13.2% for U.S. markets and 33.5% for world markets. Clearly, options trading, both stock and futures, has become an indispensable financial tool for the world's markets.

*Allen Jan Baird, *Option Market Making* (New York: John Wiley & Sons).

TABLE 2.1
U.S. COMMODITY EXCHANGES

Chicago Board of Trade
Chicago Mercantile Exchange
Commodity Exchange, New York
Chicago Rice and Cotton Exchange
Coffee, Sugar and Cocoa Exchange, New York
Kansas City Board of Trade
Minneapolis Grain Exchange
Mid-America Exchange
New York Cotton Exchange
New York Futures Exchange
New York Mercantile Exchange

Commodities Traded

Barley
Broilers (frozen and chilled)
Cocoa
Coffee
Corn
Corn syrup
Cotton
Domestic feed barley
Domestic feed oat
Domestic feed wheat
Feeder cattle
High-fructose corn syrup
Live cattle
Live hogs
Lumber
Oats
Orange juice
Pigs
Pork bellies
Potatoes
Potato starch
Rapeseed
Red beans
Rough rice
Rye
Shrimp
Soybean meal
Soybean oil
Soybeans
Sugar
Wheat

Most people never realize how many everyday products are traded on some commodity exchanges. We have all heard jokes about pork bellies, and cattle futures, but did you know chicken (broilers), corn syrup, and barley are also traded? When you consider what is traded on the world's market, nursery trees do not sound very far-fetched. Table 2.1 lists both the U.S. commodity exchanges and the commodities traded on the world's markets. The list excludes many financial and currency contracts, such as Treasury bills and Eurodollars, as well as metals' contracts, such as aluminum, copper, nickel, gold, and silver.

3

SME Trading Structure and Exercise Procedures

COMPUTERIZED TRADING AT SME

Unlike commodity exchanges where floor traders conduct business by screaming at one another in a pit, SME uses the National Computerized Trading System (NCTS) developed by the exchange. NCTS allows member brokers to initiate trades for their clients directly. With the advent of computer technology, NCTS is cost efficient, accurate, and more important, fast. NCTS has all the elements of floor trading except the physical trading.

The exchange tradition of trading in pits (stepped circular arenas), where buyers and sellers met to argue price, dates back several centuries. Many people believed that this "open-out cry" allowed for honest and efficient price discovery. Given the technology of the day, open-out cry in a centralized market made sense. With today's technology, however, pit trading can be eliminated. It seems, however, that traditions within exchanges die hard; change is always difficult to accept, even when it is productive.

Although computers drive exchanges, over the years they were mostly relegated to back-office operations. Currently, however, exchanges and brokerage firms are moving aggressively to automate order taking and placing. It is estimated that 30% to 40% of all orders now placed on the world's markets are moved by computer. With the development of on-line computer services, orders from consumers and institutional buyers can be sent electronically to the trading desk on the floor of most major exchanges. There the order is run to the pits for a match. This development eliminates having to telephone a broker, who must then send the order to the in-house order entry staff, who then call the order into the trading desk on the floor of the exchange.

Obviously, computers have improved order processing time, have cut paper flow, and have allowed for the ultimate objective, increased trade volume, from which exchanges and brokers derive their revenue. It will, however, be years, if ever, before the pits are closed and are replaced by computer screens matching orders.

There is also movement towards electronic trading. The Global Exchange (GLOBEX) is revolutionizing the world's markets. GLOBEX, developed by the Chicago Mercantile Exchange, the Chicago Board of Trade, and Reuters Holdings PLC, the world's largest telecommunication entity, is an electronic trading system currently operating on various exchanges. The system supports 24-hour a day world trading. According to those involved with GLOBEX, it will ultimately be the central trading system for all the world's futures and option markets. Billed as a system that trades when the U.S. exchanges are closed, its real purpose is to curtail the U.S. exchanges' loss of trade volume to other world markets. GLOBEX does offer order matching; therefore, it is capable of eliminating the open-out cry, which is expensive for exchanges to maintain and not very efficient. Given that thousands are employed by exchanges to support the pits, only time and a lot of persuasion will show if electronic trading will be fully utilized.

SME's birth in the era of technology offered the opportunity to be on the cutting edge of electronic trading. With electronic trading, brokers have no idea who their order will be matched with; therefore, better security against possible trader collusion is achieved. In addition, electronic trading is more efficient than traditional methods. Through consistent monitoring of the trades, exchange personnel can spot potential problems. It is, if you will, a blind system for trading, with the exchange ensuring the trade and the clearinghouse guaranteeing the trade.

The integrity of the market is of utmost concern; thus the SME has strived to develop a system that not only conducts trades but also the means to settle those trades effectively. NCTS trading offers an open, efficient, and competitive auction market.

GUARANTEED CONTRACT PERFORMANCE

The SME Clearing House guarantees that the terms of an option contract will be honored. All trading clients have direct accounts with the clearinghouse, and all material traded on the exchange is done by a "pool," supplied by member growers and governed by the clearinghouse. The essential purpose of the clearinghouse is to guarantee performance to all market participants. The clearinghouse takes no active position in the market, but interposes itself between all parties to every transaction. It serves this role when a buy-and-sell trade relationship is established on the exchange.

The clearinghouse resolves all potential transaction difficulties. Once the clearinghouse is satisfied that there are matching orders from a buyer and a seller, it severs the link between the parties. In effect, the clearinghouse becomes the buyer to the seller and the seller to the buyer, thereby guaranteeing contract performance.

As a result, the seller can buy back the same option he or she has written, closing out the initial transaction and terminating an obligation, such as to deliver the underlying commodity to the clearinghouse. This in no way affects the right of the original buyer to sell, hold, or exercise his or her option. All settlement payments are made to, and paid by, the clearinghouse, not the buyer to seller as on the cash market. This settlement procedure, the founding principal of all exchanges, guarantees to all parties prompt and timely payment. It also eliminates the serious receivable aging (now 63 days) problem currently affecting the nursery industry's cash flow.

Growers selected to supply material to the pool must meet very strict supply standards. First, underwriters (members of the SME) interview growers about their history in the industry, client satisfaction, industry affiliations, and so on, to determine the financial stability of growers as well as the quality consistency of their products. Not all growers interviewed are accepted to supply material to the pool. In fact, the majority are not.

After approval by the underwriters, growers must then be approved by the SME Clearing House. The SME can, for whatever reason, reject a grower. For example, the SME may have information regarding a grower that the underwriter did not. The SME makes the final decision.

Underwriters and growers who supply material to the clearinghouse pool are contractually bound to perform. Those supplying nursery material to the clearinghouse pool are issued a clearinghouse nursery material receipt (NMR) (Figure 3.1), which secures the material the underwriter or growers desire to have sold on the forward market.

Once a grower is accepted to supply material and has developed a history for delivery, he or she can apply for permanent exchange membership. Underwriters, in the final analysis, are financially responsible for the performance of all growers that they recommend to SME. Therefore, an underwriter has a vested interest to ensure that a grower recommended by that underwriter will fulfill specific obligations, such as delivery of quality product when needed. Accepting questionable growers is not in the best interest of SME.

Nursery Stock Grading Standards

The grading and quality of nursery stock are issues with which the industry has long contended. For example, there are at least five definitions of *spread* and countless definitions of *canopy*. After numerous conversations with industry professionals, the SME decided to adopt the standards set by the American Association of Nurserymen (AAN). Therefore, SME contracts for grading of deliverable material are modeled after the AAN's published works.

The deliverable grades of nursery stock traded on the exchange are concurrent with the standards outlined in the American Standard for Nursery Stock (ASNS), published by the American Association of Nurserymen, Inc.*

Although descriptions of the options and forward contracts traded are contained in this book, SME contract specifications, available from a broker or the exchange directly, should be reviewed.

Field Inspection for Delivery on a Forward Contract

The nursery industry has long been plagued with growers or wholesalers who do not, intentionally or otherwise, ship exactly what the buyer expected and purchased. To ensure that an SME buyer receives what was expected, the SME guarantees that the material being shipped meets exact SME contract specifications. If a contract calls for 100 1" caliper, 4' high, 5' wide units, then that is exactly what the buyer receives.

When an option is exercised to a forward contract and delivery is scheduled, SME horticulture personnel are on hand at the delivery site during the loading process. This ensures that the material being shipped meets or exceeds SME contract specifications. If the material does not meet the specifications, it is rejected for shipment. Moreover, material meeting specifications must be loaded before the grower receives payment. SME personnel inspecting the material must sign off on the shipment, prior to and after loading. They are present for the entire process.

*For a copy of the standards, contact the AAN at 1250 I St. NW, Suite 500, Washington, DC 20005 (telephone: 202-789-2900).

Seattle Mercantile Exchange Clearing House
Nursery Material Receipt (NMR)
(European)

SME

(1) Nursery Material Description

Genus		(circle one) Grading Method	Size at Delivery
Species		A) Container	
Variety		B) Caliper	
SME Symbol		C) Height	
Total Quantity		D) Spread	
Closed Harvest of Total Qty		Root Form	
Delivery Month/Year	Price Per Plant	Add $ for Closed Harvest	
May			
November			
May			
November			
May			
November			
Material Delivery Location			

(2) Seattle Mercantile Exchange Clearing House (hence forth referred to as "Clearing House") issues Nursery Material Receipts (NMR) to Producers of nursery material that desire to supply nursery material to the Clearing House "pool" from which options and their underlying forward contracts are written and offered for trade on the Seattle Mercantile Exchange. The undersigned (also referred to as PRODUCER) desires to supply nursery material, as described in paragraph (1), to the Clearing House "pool" and hereby agrees to supply material as called for by the terms and conditions contained herein. Neither the Seattle Mercantile Exchange, nor the Clearing House, take ownership of material supplied the "pool". It is understood by PRODUCER, the Clearing House makes no representations that material covered under this NMR will be placed under option, exercised to a forward contract or sold. All items pertaining to settlement of obligations covered by this NMR are as set forth herein. Should the material for which this NMR secures be sold through Seattle Mercantile Exchange efforts, the price paid to PRODUCER and quantities to be delivered by PRODUCER, are as stated in paragraph (1). Further, all material offered by PRODUCER to satisfy PRODUCER obligations contained in this NMR must satisfy Seattle Mercantile Exchange contract specifications.

(3) Now therefore, Seattle Mercantile Exchange will offer for trading, covered call options and forward contracts on material secured by this NMR. The Clearing House will notify the undersigned when the Clearing House desires to have the undersigned make delivery of the material described herein. The undersigned agrees to make delivery of, at any time during the contract's delivery month, under the terms contained, the nursery material described herein.

(4) PRODUCER hereby represents that it is the sole owner of material described herein, and that PRODUCER has full right and title, and has the authority to transfer same to the Clearing House, its agent, and/or a holder of a forward contract. Producer authorizes Seattle Mercantile Exchange and/or Seattle Mercantile Exchange Clearing House personnel or agents to inspect any growing operation,

Figure 3.1 Seattle Mercantile Exchange Clearing House Nursery Material Receipt (NMR)

warehouse or field site that producer represents as a location(s) of an issued NMR's underlying commodity.

(5) During the period the material is listed with the Clearing House "pool", or during the period the material is under option, PRODUCER does not relinquish its ownership rights and title to the nursery material described herein. However, pending final Clearing House disposition of the material, PRODUCER agrees not to sell, trade, barter or transfer, in any manner, the rights and title to said material, be it physical or otherwise.

(6) **Delivery of material**: Clearing House horticulturists will inspect, and have the authority to reject any and all material the PRODUCER offers to satisfy its obligations as described in this NMR that does not meet contract specifications or quality standards. PRODUCER is responsible for loading approved material onto a Clearing House scheduled delivery vehicle at a mutually accepted site. PRODUCER'S obligations end when the material as described herein is loaded onto said delivery vehicle, and PRODUCER is thereafter released from all obligations contained in this NMR. All funds to purchase said material are held by the Clearing House, and are released the next business day after the time the material is loaded (make delivery).

(7) **Default and remedies:** If, when notified by the Clearing House to make delivery, PRODUCER shall be unable to deliver to the Clearing House any commodity sold by the Clearing House, subject to this NMR, PRODUCER authorizes the Clearing House, in its discretion, to borrow or to buy the like commodity from any other source to make delivery thereof, and PRODUCER shall pay and indemnify the Clearing House for any cost, loss, and damage (including consequential costs, losses, and damages) which the Clearing House may sustain thereby and any premiums which the Clearing House may be required to pay thereon, and for any cost, loss, and damage (including consequential costs, losses, and damages) which the Clearing House may sustain thereby and any premiums which the Clearing House maybe required to pay thereon, and for any cost, loss, and damage (including consequential costs, losses, and damages) which the Clearing House may sustain from its inability to borrow or buy any such commodity. Further, PRODUCER hereby releases the Clearing House from any cost, loss, and damage (including consequential costs, losses, and damages) which the PRO-DUCER may sustain due to non-performance of any item contained herein, by a Clearing House vendor, its employees, agents, and/or their ancillary vendors.

(8) **Succession of NMR:** Including all authorizations, shall inure to the benefit of the Clearing House, its successors, assigns and trustees and shall be binding upon PRODUCER and PRODUCER's personal representatives, executors, trustees, administrators, agents, successors and assigns.

(9) **Venue:** All actions or proceedings arising directly, indirectly or otherwise in connection with, out of, related to, or from this NMR or any transaction covered hereby shall be governed by the law of the State of Washington and shall, at the discretion and election of the Clearing House, be litigated in courts situated in the State of Washington.

(10) **Understandings:** The signing of this NMR constitutes a contract and PRODUCER agrees to all terms and conditions as outlined herein, the rules and regulations of the Seattle Mercantile Exchange, the Clearing House and Member Broker agreements.

Producer (Nursery) _____ _____ Phone _____

Mailing Address _____

Authorized Signature_____ Title_____ Date _____

Signature _____ Title_____ Date _____
Authorized Agent for Seattle Mercantile Exchange Clearing House

Should a grower attempt to undermine the integrity of the inspection, his or her SME trading and supply privileges are terminated. There is no appeal process. Obviously, it is not in the growers' financial interest to circumvent this important procedure. In the unlikely event that unacceptable material (not meeting contract specs) is shipped, the buyer has recourse with the exchange. In addition, the buyer's broker is a strong advocate.

Guarantees regarding shipment follow customary and prevailing industry standards. Selection of a shipper is the responsibility of the buyer, as is the cost of shipping. SME and the grower, however, can assist with choosing a shipper. Shipping procedures can be discussed with a broker, who can assist with final shipping arrangements.

The inspection advantage alone illustrates why trading with SME makes sense. A buyer will not be concerned with what is unloaded from a truck. SME obligations are to the integrity of the market, and the better growers understand and appreciate that. Clearly, SME procedures for nursery stock inspection and guarantees exceed the current shipping procedures for cash market transactions. Shipping quality product is a sensitive issue within the industry. Therefore, the SME and underwriters, growers, and brokers strive to ensure quality as it is in the best interest of everyone in the industry.

TYPES OF OPTIONS

Call Options

A call option is a contract that conveys to its holder the right, but not the obligation, to buy a forward contract at a specified price on or before a given date. This right is granted by the seller of the option. A put option (described in Chapter 10) obligates the holder to sell a forward contract at a predetermined price. A put option is not the opposite transaction of a call option; they are both different options that serve two very distinct functions.

Forward Contracts

A forward contract is one of the oldest marketing alternatives available to allow the buyer and seller to know the price of the forward contract's underlying commodity prior to actual delivery. It is a binding transaction between buyer and seller, where certain conditions have been negotiated and set. These conditions are quantity, grading method, delivery time, place, and price. One SME forward contract represents 25 trees.

An analogy of a forward contract is a purchase order. As quantity, quality, delivery, and so forth are spelled out in a purchase order, so are the terms and conditions of a forward contract. The price for a forward contract's underlying commodity, when offered on the primary market, is collectively determined by the exchange, underwriters, and member growers. If you own (purchase) a forward contract, however, you can, on the secondary market, sell the contract for whatever the market is willing to pay. (Forward contract pricing is discussed later in this chapter).

A forward contract option allows a buyer to secure, for a price, the right for a specific period of time at which a forward contract can be purchased. Buyers and sellers on the secondary market can determine what each will pay or receive for that right. Such leverage means that by using options one is not only able to increase the potential benefit from the nursery stock's price movements on the cash market, but also can purchase the right to secure inventory for delivery at a later date. The advantages of those two important aspects of an option's flexibility are explained in detail throughout this book.

The ability to plan cash for inventory purchases is by far the most important aspect of trading options. Given the current banking climate, as inventory capital becomes increasingly difficult to obtain, options trading offers the ultimate in cash flow flexibility. Moreover, options offer the buyer the ability to secure large amounts of inventory at a fraction of the cost of securing inventory on the cash market.

Option Contract Size

Except under special circumstances, all forward option contracts are for one forward contract for 25 trees of the same size and grade of the underlying nursery stock. The strike price of an option is the specified price at which the nursery material will be bought or sold if the holder exercises his or her option. Strike prices, depending on the market price of the underlying material, are listed in increments of $1, or points ($1 per point). Most often, forward contract strike prices are at a few levels above or below the current cash market price.

Depending on the value of a forward contract's strike price, option contracts may be sold in minimum lots. For example, to satisfy minimum requirements, four option contracts representing four forward contracts for 25 trees per contract may need to be purchased. Typically, forward contracts with strike prices of less than $100 (price per tree) are most often available in minimum lots of 100, or four option contracts.

Other than long-term options (up to 3 years), a particular option with one of two expiration dates within the year can be bought at any given time. Those expiration dates are in April and October, with delivery months of the forward contract in May and November, respectively. As a result of this standardization, option prices can be obtained quickly and easily at any time during trading hours. In addition, closing option premium and forward contract prices are published in various print and broadcast media.

Flexibility

Options are extremely versatile. Because of their unique risk and reward structure, options can be used in many combinations with other option contracts to create either a hedged or speculative position. Some basic strategies are described in Chapter 10.

Options share many similarities with common stocks, or other commodity exchange–traded contracts. Both options and forward contracts are tradable contracts. Orders to buy and sell options are handled through brokers, members of the exchange, in the same way as orders to buy and sell stocks are. Like stocks, options are traded with buyers making bids and sellers making offers. In stocks, those bids and offers are for shares of stock. In SME options, they are for the right to buy or sell a forward contract.

Option buyers, like stock investors, have the ability to follow price movements, trading volume, and other pertinent information day by day or even minute by minute. The buyer or seller of an option can quickly learn the price at which his or her order has been executed. Although options and common stocks are quite similar, some important differences should be noted.

Unlike common stock, an option has a limited life. Common stock can be held indefinitely in the hope that its value may increase, while every option has an expiration date. If an option is not closed out (sold) or exercised prior to its expiration date, it ceases to exist as a financial instrument. For this reason, an option is considered a "wasting asset."

As stated, an option is simply a contract involving a buyer willing to pay a price to obtain certain rights and a seller willing to grant these rights in return for the price. Thus, unlike shares of common stock, the number of outstanding options (commonly referred to as "open interest") depends solely on the number of buyers and sellers interested in receiving and conferring these rights.

A fixed number of options are available on the SME, based on the quantity of nursery stock the SME Clearing House makes available for the SME to trade. This quantity is determined by many factors, such as the supply available from growers and the quantity the clearinghouse will release based on market stability and open interest.

Stocks have certificates evidencing their ownership; options do not. Option positions are indicated on printed statements prepared by a buyer's or seller's brokerage firm. Certificateless trading, an innovation of the option markets, sharply reduces paperwork and delays.

AMERICAN AND EUROPEAN STYLES OF OPTIONS

There are two styles of options: American and European. In an American option, the holder of an option has the right to exercise his or her option on or before the expiration date of the option; otherwise, the option will expire worthless and will cease to exist as a financial instrument. A European option is an option that can only be exercised upon its expiration. The holder or writer of either style of option can close out his or her position at any time simply by making an offsetting, or closing, transaction.

A closing transaction is one in which, at some point prior to expiration, the buyer of an option trades (sells) his or her option. The writer (one who supplies material) of an option must make an offsetting purchase of an identical option and let the option expire. This closing transaction cancels the writer's obligation to make delivery of the forward contract's underlying commodity. Removing material committed to the forward market is explained in detail later in Chapter 6. The SME trades options of both American and European style. Both styles are offered by the SME primarily because of the nursery stock availability. Growers inform the clearinghouse about the material available that they wish to offer for sale on the forward market and the date that the material can be shipped. Unlike other commodities such as corn or wheat that can be stored easily, some material cannot be harvested and shipped during certain periods of the year, nor can it be stored indefinitely. For buyers and sellers alike to accommodate the market, the SME has established trading for both types of options. When placing orders with a broker, both buyers and sellers must make sure that they clearly understand the style of option wanted.

THE OPTION CONTRACT

An option contract is defined by the following elements: type (put or call), style (American or European), underlying forward contract unit of trade (number of trees), strike price, and expiration date. All option contracts that are of the same type and style and cover the same underlying forward contract are referred to as a class of options. All options of the same class that also have the same unit of trade at the same strike price and expiration date are referred to as an option series. See Figure 3.2 for an example of an option contract.

If a person's interest in a particular series of options is as a net holder (that is, if the number of contracts bought

OPTIONS ON

Fagus sylvatica
(European Beech)

FORWARD CONTRACTS

Trading Unit: One SME contract (of a specified contract month) of a minimum 25 trees.

Tick Size: $1.00 (minimum price fluctuation)

Strike price: Market

Daily Price Limit: Limits may be established.

Contract Months: April, October

Contract Year: January through December

Last Trading Day: Seventh business day preceding the expire date.

Exercise: The holder of a forward option may exercise the option on any business day prior to expiration date by giving notice to SME Clearing House by 10:00am Seattle Time. Option exercise results in an underlying forward contract position

Expiration Date: Unexercised options expire at 1:00pm Seattle time on the last business day of the contract month.

Trading Hours: 7:00am - 1:00pm Seattle time, Monday through Friday.

Ticker Symbol: FGSSL

Figure 3.2 Sample Option Contract

exceeds the number of contracts sold), then this person has a long position in the series. Likewise, if a person's interest in a particular series of options is as a net writer (if the number of contracts sold exceeds the number of contracts bought), he or she is said to have a short position in the series.

Placing an Option Order

Orders to buy or sell are generated by SME member brokerage firms. Brokerage firms are independently owned and operated and have full trading and settlement privileges with the SME. Say that a nursery wholesaler wants to buy a call option for a particular material type for a certain delivery date. To place an order, the wholesaler simply telephones his or her brokerage firm and tells the firm what is needed. The brokerage firm, in turn, inquires with the exchange, through the NCTS, about option contract month availability, option premium, and the strike price of the underlying forward contract. The brokerage firm then provides this information to the wholesaler, who decides whether or not to take a position (buy the option) in the market.

Once a trade is consummated, the clearinghouse issues a confirmation of the trade for settlement to the client, with a copy to the broker. The client must settle (make payment) within 7 days from the time the trade is consummated. If settlement is not made (failed trade), the client's broker is responsible for settlement; the broker will then seek recourse with the client. For details regarding settlement procedure, refer to a broker's client contracts.

To trade, the SME client (as with clients of any other exchange) must open a trading account. Brokers will supply the client with the necessary agreements (acceptable to the SME) to open an account. Given that the SME trades only on a cash basis, the client does not have to open a margin account (deposit). Therefore, because a deposit is not necessary to open an account, a client can simply contact a broker; ask him or her to forward an account application, fill it out, and return it to the broker. This can be done at any time; a person does not need to be interested in trading now to have an open active account.

In addition to supplying account applications, a broker will supply an SME disclosure document. This information outlines the terms and conditions by which the SME trades and covers all settlement procedures. The broker will also supply a commission rate schedule. Commissions vary from broker to broker, and rates vary based on the client's trading volume. But like anything else, service from the broker should be used as a deciding factor. Some brokers offer in-depth market analysis, while others assume that clients know the market and need little, if any, advice. Therefore, clients should inform brokers of exactly the type of information and advice needed.

Moreover, a broker is trained to work with clients, their accountants, and others who may have purchasing or inventory responsibilities for the clients. A broker's expertise to develop a trading program based on a client's particular inventory or hedging requirements is necessary. Most brokers offer spreadsheet analyses to assist in inventory planning. Clients should ask brokers for help; commissions pay for that assistance.

Exercising the Option

If the holder of an option decides to exercise his or her right to buy (in the case of a call) or to sell (in the case of a put) the underlying nursery stock, the holder must direct his or her broker to submit an exercise notice to the clearinghouse. To ensure that an option is exercised on a particular day, the holder must notify the broker before the broker's cut-off time for accepting exercise instructions on that day. Different firms may have different cut-off times for accepting exercise instructions from customers. Notwithstanding the brokers requirements, the SME has established expiration dates. Refer to SME contract specifications for those and other important procedures.

Upon receipt of an exercise notice, the clearinghouse will then randomly assign this exercise notice to one or more underwriters. The assigned writer will then be obligated to sell (in the case of a call) or buy (in the case of a put) the underlying forward contracts to or from the clearinghouse at the specified strike price. (Remember that the clearinghouse acts as the intermediary to ensure delivery of the forward contract or settlement amount to the holder who exercised his or her option or sold the option.)

Special Limited Contracts

The SME may offer, from time to time, contracts on select, limited-availability nursery material. When this occurs, contract specifications are available to the market. Member brokers notify clients when special contracts become available.

The Expiration Process

An option usually begins trading months before its expiration date. As a result of the growers' needs and biological restraints, however, some options have a life of only 1 to 2 months. As mentioned, an option trades on one of two expiration months throughout the year. At any given time an option can be bought or sold, as often as the market desires, prior to the option's expiration date, as designated in SME contract specifications. Options can be purchased up to 3 years. This maximum time allows both buyer and seller of nursery stock maximum hedging opportunities.

The expiration date is the last day an option exists. On the SME, this is the last business day of the contract month—April and October—with delivery months on forward contracts in May and November. The last day an option can be traded is the seventh business day preceding the expire date. This is the deadline by which brokerage firms must submit exercise notices to the clearinghouse; the SME and brokerage firms, however, have rules and procedures regarding the deadlines an option holder must notify a brokerage firm of an intention to exercise. Specific deadlines can be obtained from brokers. Most firms require their customers to notify the firm of any intention to exercise, even if an option is in the money (has value).

Underlying Forward Contract

The specific forward contract on which an option contract is based is commonly referred to as the underlying instrument. Because an option's value is derived in part from the value and characteristics of the underlying instrument (forward contract), options are categorized as derivatives. An option contract's unit of trade is the number of trees of the underlying forward contract that are represented by that option. Figure 3.3 shows a sample forward contract.

Strike Price

The strike, or exercise, price of an option is the specified price at which the trees can be bought or sold by the buyer

FORWARD CONTRACT

Fagus sylvatica
(European Beech)

Trading Unit:	25 trees, minimum
Grading Method:	Caliper
Deliverable Sizes:	1 to 4 inch
Deliverable Root Forms:	Balled & Burlapped, Bareroot, Container/Box-grown, Balled and Potted and Grow Bag.
Grading Standards:	ASNS, ANSI Z60.1-1990, Section 1* (Shade & Flowering Trees) as it applies to Type 2 (Shade Trees) for the root form delivered.
	*Only nursury grown material is supplied. Substitutions of differentials established by the Exchange.
Price Qoute:	Market
Tick Size:	$5.00 (minimum price fluctuation)
Daily Trading Limits:	Limits may be established.
Contract Months:	May, November
Contract Year:	Open Harvest, Closed Harvest
Last Trading Day:	Fifth business day preceding the first business day of the contract month.
Last Delivery Day:	Up to 31 days following the first business day of the contract month (delivery is also up to 31 days following a take delivery notification to SME Clearing House).
Trading Hours:	7:00am - 1:00pm Seattle time, Monday through Friday.
Ticker Symbol:	FGSSL

Figure 3.3 Sample Forward Contract

of the option contract, if he or she exercises the right against a seller of the option. To exercise an option is to exercise the right to buy (in the case of a call) or sell (in the case of a put) the underlying trees at the specified strike price of the option.

Underwriters

Nursery material for which options and forward contracts are traded on the SME is supplied to the clearinghouse by underwriters. Underwriters work primarily with growers who seek to have their material sold on the exchange. Underwriters are paid a fee, typically 5% to 10% of the primary option premium when the primary options are sold.

Underwriters do not receive payment on options sold on the secondary market. The primary option premium is set by underwriters, typically at the same price options are trading for the day the option is introduced.

The SME plays an active role in the introduction of primary options in that it ensures that options are not priced undermarket when introduced. This procedure maintains market integrity for options held by others (open interest). On the other hand, however, option premium on the secondary market is discovered by buyers and sellers (market). Option premium pricing, for both the primary and secondary markets, is explained in Chapter 9.

There is no cost to growers supplying material to the exchange. In fact, growers receive a percentage of the option premium revenue when options are introduced and sold on the primary market. In addition to receiving option premium, growers receive at least 15% to 20% more for their material on the forward market than on the cash market. Moreover, when material is sold on the forward market, growers are paid when they satisfy delivery requirements of a forward contract. This means that growers are paid within 24 hours of loading. Payments to growers on cash market sales currently average 63 days.

Option Premium Distribution

As an example, growers place only their excess material on the forward market. Excess material is material not shipped because of canceled cash market orders or because a client scales back an order. SME research suggests that growers' excess inventory averages 5% to 8% annually. Assume that the material has a forward market value of $250,000 and that options covering this material have a value of $30,000. Depending on the financial relationship a grower had with his or her underwriter, the grower would receive 40% ($12,000), at minimum, of the option premium when the options sold.

The grower retains the premium, regardless of the option holder exercising to a forward contract. In fact, once the options expire, the grower could introduce the same material on the exchange and receive option premium. This situation could occur over and over. Therefore, an option premium acts as a hedge for a grower to offset any lost revenue from sales on the cash market.

Contract Settlement

Unlike commodity and stock trades that are mostly conducted on a margin account basis, the SME only allows brokers to open cash accounts. A margin account is when a client can purchase stocks, for example, on credit. The client deposits cash or equivalent security—typically 10–15% of the planned trading volume—with a broker. Minimum margin requirements are set by the exchange.

Brokers, however, set their rates depending on the client's resources. The greater the client risk, the higher the margin.

As stated earlier, the role of the clearinghouse is to ensure settlement of both buyer and seller. This is accomplished by the established cash settlement procedures. Settlement guidelines are continuous net settlement (CNS) on options and trade for trade (TFT) on forward contracts. CNS means that regardless of a buyer's settlement default on an option contract, the clearinghouse makes payment to the seller. TFT on forward contracts means that when a buyer exercises his or her option to a forward contract, the buyer must deposit the entire amount due on the forward contract with the clearinghouse to secure the underlying trees. These funds are held by the SME pending the grower's delivery. Once the grower makes delivery (loading), payment is released to the grower, typically within 24 hours.

The clearinghouse acts as clearing, collection, and trust agent, and all option and forward contract funds are held pending settlement. All client option and forward contract settlements must be mailed or wired to this settlement account. The SME then distributes funds to growers, underwriters, brokers, and sellers. Funds held for grower delivery settlement are released only when the loading of the forward contracts underlying commodity is completed. Therefore, only when funds are received in full settlement from the buyer for a forward contract are trees released. There is no exception to this rule.

Example: Once an option trade is made, the clearinghouse mails a confirmation of the trade to the buyer. The buyer has 7 days to make payment. Should the buyer not make payment (settlement), the buyer's broker is ultimately responsible for the client's trading. Therefore, brokers, in their best interest and for settlement integrity, insure the client's financial resources.

Leverage

A call option, as stated, gives its holder the right to buy an underlying forward contract, whereas a put option conveys the right to sell an underlying forward contract.

For example, an American-style April 1994 50 call entitles the buyer to purchase a forward contract of 25 trees at $50 per tree at any time prior to the option's April expiration date. Likewise, an American-style April 1994 50 put entitles the buyer to sell 25 trees at $50 per tree at any time prior to the option's April expiration date.

For example, to own 25 black pines selling on the cash market at $50 per tree would cost $1,250. On the other hand, owning a $5 call option with a strike price of $50 would give you the right to buy 25 black pines for $50 per tree at any time during the life of the option; this would cost only $125. Remember that premiums are quoted on a per contract basis; thus a $5 premium represents a premium payment of $5 × 25 (the number of trees in the forward contract) = $125 per option contract.

Now assume that 1 month after the option contract was purchased, the cash market price for black pines rose to $55 per tree. For those holding trees on the cash market, the gain is $125, or 10%. For the same $5 increase in the cash market price, however, the call option premium might increase to $7, for a return of $50 ($2 × $25), or 40% on the $125 original option investment.

Leverage also has downside. If the cash market does not rise as anticipated, or if it falls during the life of the option, leverage will magnify the investment's percentage loss. For instance, if the price of black pines had fallen to

$40 per tree, this $10 decrease in the cash market price would cause the option value to decrease 20%. Note that the most an option buyer can lose is the premium amount paid for the option contract. On the other hand, if you purchased black pine on the cash market at $50, and the cash market decreased to $40 per tree, the inventory's value would decrease by $250.

Limited Risk for Buyers

Unlike owning the trees outright, or other investments where the risks have no limit, options offer a known risk to buyers. An option buyer absolutely cannot lose more than the price of the option, the premium. Because the right to buy or sell the underlying forward contract at a specific price expires on a given date, the option will expire worthless if the conditions for profitable exercise or sale of the contract are not met by the expiration date.

4

Cash Market Issues

THE LOCAL CASH MARKET

The local cash market price refers to the price at which a grower can sell material, or the price at which a buyer can purchase material on the cash market (sometimes referred to as spot market). The terms *cash* or *spot market* mean "at that moment." Perhaps *the* most important relationship to understand is the continuous and constantly changing relationship between cash market prices and forward market prices.

The necessity to understand such relationships is by no means limited to growers. Nursery material merchandising has become an increasingly complex and competitive business in which shrewd buying and selling is a prerequisite for success and even survival. All segments—landscape brokers, landscape contractors, landscape architects, and others—can similarly guide themselves toward effective marketing and buying strategies by translating market understanding into market profits.

In addition to issues raised in Chapter 1, the nursery material cash market is currently dominated by a stratified cost-plus pricing strategy. For example, growers sell to rewholesalers, who sell to wholesalers, who sell to garden centers, landscape contractors, and other industry professionals. Operating throughout this chain are the landscape brokers, looking to market material wherever and whenever needed.

Although variations to this chain certainly occur, the one constant in the process is a price mark-up at each level (cost-plus, with an industry average of approximately 40%). Should individuals further along in the distribution system, such as landscape contractors, attempt to circumvent this structure (and price increase) by purchasing material directly from a grower, they may encounter higher prices than those charged to wholesalers or landscape brokers.

In short, price discrimination reduces the motivation to eliminate dealers. More important, this structure has a negative effect on the most critical element of the chain, the growers. Without confidence in price development, few growers will be motivated to produce and mature the variety of materials needed in landscape design.

Although the current cash market structure adequately distributes nursery material, the existing techniques for pricing and marketing are often financially inefficient. Moreover, at times, dealing with the structure can be frustrating for all those involved. The lack of price integrity or consistency fosters distrust between buyers and sellers, and the industry standard of different prices for different segments forces buyers into protracted negotiations to ensure a reasonable price for material. Also, cost-plus pricing policies tend to mask the transportation costs and regional market differences, and they completely ignore true value to the grower.

LOCAL MARKET ALTERNATIVES

As everyone knows, growers can sell material during or after harvest. But making the right decision, at the right time, is not particularly easy. If growers are familiar with the various cash market alternatives and how each alternative works, they will be able to make informed decisions that best serve their marketing needs.

VARIOUS CASH MARKET ALTERNATIVES

The nursery industry is not short of methods to sell material. To receive or pay a price that is fair and equitable to all parties is, however, difficult to establish. Various alternatives to cash markets are discussed below. Forward markets are designed to eliminate most, if not all, of the inequity present in the cash market.

Established Price List

An established price list means delivering material at some future date at a price previously determined. This commonly used method leaves the grower open to both price-level risk and basis risk. With a price list established months before delivery, the grower cannot take advantage of possible increased prices. Moreover, this alternative does not guarantee delivery.

Cash Sale

Cash sales, or delivering material to the cash market and receiving a price that day, is the most common marketing alternative to established price lists. By using this alternative, however, growers are open to price-level risk and basis risk. With a cash sale, the selling price is established on the day the material is delivered. Growers can take advantage of higher prices and a strong basis; or they may be subject to lower prices and a weak basis, depending on current market conditions. Conversely, buyers are subject to the same adverse conditions.

Storage

Another marketing alternative, used in conjunction with the cash market, is to store material on-site. Growers can benefit from storing the material and, at a later date, sell the material on the cash or forward markets. One general rule applies to both markets, however: growers should store only when the return to storage is greater than the cost of storage. Knowledge of markets, historical basis, and storage costs helps growers make this marketing decision. With storage, growers still have to assume both the price level and basis risk, but the marketing period is longer and there is often more flexibility.

Prepurchase Agreement

In a prepurchase agreement, the material's price and delivery dates are set. Settlement is sometime in the future. The grower negotiates, up front, quantity, price, and deposits with the buyer. The delivery date is typically 90 to 120 days from the order date, and deposits do not always cover the material's related basis. In addition, the grower receives little, if any, of the material's appreciation. Moreover, should a buyer have financial problems, the grower keeps the deposits but needs to find another buyer.

Contract Growing

In contract growing, the grower assigns to a buyer a select number of acres to grow a particular type of material. The buyer assumes all costs associated with the material development, and the grower limits his or her revenue to the amount the buyer contracts for each acre.

Delayed Pricing

Delayed pricing is a cash market alternative that allows the grower to deliver and price the material at the same time. The grower and the buyer negotiate a future delivery date; the price for the material is based on specific market conditions on the prearranged delivery date. Upon delivery, the title to the material is transferred to the buyer. With this alternative, the grower is subject to changes in price and basis levels.

Fundamental to understanding current cash market behavior is realizing that growers have no means of determining the true value of their material. Without this basic starting point, growers have little guidance (outside of historical cost data) in setting their local cash market prices. This forces growers into a policy of "scavenger pricing": Knowing what price the buyer can get for the material dictates what price the growers are charged. If growers were supplied with a true value for their material, they would be able to price more efficiently. This efficiency translates directly into rational and consistent pricing policies.

5

Basis Makes Up
the Difference

WHAT IS BASIS?

Basis is the amount, on any given day, that the local cash price of a commodity is above or below the nearest forward contract price for a particular delivery period (local cash price − forward contract price = basis.) The components of basis can be divided into two general categories. The first, the fixed category, is a one-time addition to basis. It contains, for example, costs incurred by the grower for the loading of material for shipping.

The second, or cumulative, category is so named because its components are repeatedly added to the basis as time progresses. Carrying costs, made up of maintenance, opportunity, and attributable overhead costs, accrue over time and are added to the basis at regularly established intervals. Material appreciation, defined as any increase in a material's value due to growth, artistic development, or supply/demand interaction, also accrues over time and is likewise added at regularly established intervals.

CALCULATING BASIS

Fixed basis components are calculated by analyzing information—cash market prices (price lists)—received directly from growers. Cumulative basis components are calculated by surveying a group of industry experts (landscape architects, wholesalers, growers, and so forth) and analyzing current and historical grower pricing information. Table 5.1 reviews the procedures to determine cumulative basis components.

An economic model can be used to aid in analyzing the supply/demand interaction and its effects on basis. Such a model combines factors such as construction activity, interest rates, gross national product (GNP), crop sizes, and growth influences to make predictions of prevailing market prices.

TABLE 5.1
PROCEDURES TO DETERMINE CUMULATIVE
BASIS COMPONENTS

1. An agricultural cost of production model can be used to determine the cost to grow material to various stages.
2. Maintenance costs to develop the material can be established by using agricultural production information.
3. Current and past grower price lists can be used to establish the material's typical value increase over time. After converting historical prices to current dollar prices, maintenance costs are deducted to yield the net price of maintenance costs. This price can then be used to calculate material appreciation. (See the text for an example.)
4. Resultant data from steps two and three can be used to generate a final appreciation schedule. This schedule can then be verified with general and industry-specific economic data.

Obtaining and understanding basis is as important for growers as it is for buyers of material. Without this knowledge, it would be difficult to decide the acceptance or rejection of a price for material, whether or when to store material for sale at a later date, or when to arrange for delivery.

Example: Assume that maintenance costs on a Japanese laceleaf maple were $50 per unit per year. The price lists for 1992 and 1993 are as follows:

PRICE LISTS

1992 listing		1993 listing	
Caliper	Price	Caliper	Price
1″	$100	1″	$115
2″	$200	2″	$230
3″	$350	3″	$395

Assuming, for our example only, that it takes 1 year to add 1 inch in caliper, then the 1", 2", and 3" calipers can be interpreted as successive years of growth (that is, 1" to 2" of growth takes 1 year, 2" to 3" of growth takes another year). Convert 1992 nominal prices to 1993 dollars, assuming that the inflation rate was 5%:

1992 listing (1993 dollars)		1993 listing	
Caliper	Price	Caliper	Price
1"	$105	1"	$115
2"	$210	2"	$230
3"	$370	3"	$395

AVERAGING OF PRICES YIELDS

Caliper	Price	Maintenance	Net Price of Maintenance
1"	$110	$50	$110 − $50 = $60
2"	$220	$50 + $50	$220 − $100 = $120
3"	$380	$50 + $50 + $50	$380 − $150 = $230

Thus the tree appreciates by $60 during growth from 1" to 2" and by $110 during growth from 2" to 3". (*Note:* The appreciation amounts may not be constant over time.)

LOCATION AND BASIS

Although the costs associated with elements of basis may differ, the components of basis are the same. One grower may have higher labor costs or higher land costs. When determining the material costs and the appropriate basis for a region, use a weighted average of the costs for all participating growers.

Just as basis varies among growers, basis also varies for individuals carrying inventory. In one area, inventory basis may be $80 per year per plant but $76 in another location and $84 in yet another. In each area there is obviously a different basis.

PASSAGE OF TIME AND BASIS

The predictable feature of basis is its tendency to strengthen, by the amount of reduced storage costs and increased product appreciation, as the delivery period approaches. Thus if storage costs of $45 per period and appreciation of $40 per period are included in the basis, it is likely that the basis will strengthen at the rate of $85 per period. This, of course, assumes that the other basis components remain unchanged.

Example: In 1994 period 1 (periods refer to time between contract months), the local price of a Japanese laceleaf maple at $195 is $170 under the 1995 period 1 price of $365. That is, the basis is $170. By 1994 period 2, all else remaining unchanged, the basis should strengthen to $85.

The tendency of the basis to strengthen as the delivery month approaches is known as convergence. Indeed, at the time and place of delivery, the cash price and forward contract price are normally the same. This convergence is assured because if prices were higher in the forward market than in the cash market, or vice versa, individuals would take delivery in the low-priced market or make delivery in the high-priced market, thereby quickly minimizing any price difference.

LOCAL CASH PRICES AND DISTANT FORWARD CONTRACT MONTHS

Prices for distant forward contract months differ by the amount of the current carrying charge and product appreciation. Thus if the April 1994 forward contract price of a Japanese laceleaf maple is $365 and the combined storage and relative appreciation value is $85 per period, then the October 1994 forward contract price is $450, the April 1995 forward contract price is $535, and the October 1995 forward contract price is $620. That is, forward prices usually increase incrementally.

Basis can be calculated for any forward contract month simply by subtracting the current cash market price from the price of the designated forward contract price. For example, in October 1994 the local cash price is $180 and the April 1995 forward contract price is $365, then the April 1995 basis is $185.

The basis pattern for distant delivery periods is similar to that for the nearby delivery period. That is, the basis tends to strengthen, by the amount of the reduction in carrying costs and accumulated product appreciation, as the delivery period approaches.

THE IMPORTANCE OF LOCAL BASIS

Without a knowledge of the usual basis and basis patterns for a particular area of operation, it is impossible to make fully informed decisions. For example, whether to accept or reject a given price; whether and when to store material; whether, when, and in what contract months to hedge; when to close (or "lift") a hedge; or when and how to turn an unusual basis situation into a possible profit opportunity are all extremely important issues.

BASIS RECORDS

At the very least it is useful to have a record of cash and forward market prices—and the basis difference—during those periods in which material is marketed. Nothing elaborate is necessary; a table created by dividing a sheet of lined notebook paper into vertical columns is sufficient. Keep in mind that basis is the difference between two prices. Last year's material price lists can assist in determining basis. Simply compare prices from year to year. The difference between the prices should cover the elements of basis in which the grower was interested. Although basis developed from price lists may not consider all the elements and analysis for determining basis, it is a start.

BASIS CHARTS

Basis charts are very helpful because they show patterns visually. On the other hand, tabular records of cash prices, forward market prices, and the resulting basis are also easy to maintain and use and will provide all the necessary information to track basis.

With very little additional effort, however, it is possible to keep both a tabular record and charts for those periods that are of interest. Three ways to plot a chart are worth considering:

1. Plot actual cash and forward market prices on the same chart. The difference between them is the basis. This approach has the advantage of showing dollar price levels as well as the basis. The disadvantage is that variations in the basis may not be readily apparent.

2. Plot the local cash price in dollars per unit below the forward market price, which is set at zero. The basis point will be the amount that the cash price is above or below the forward market price. This method does not show the actual level of prices, but it does reveal even small fluctuations in the basis pattern and shows the basis pattern visually.

3. Set the local cash price at zero. Plot the forward price in dollars per unit above (or below) the local cash price. This method's advantage is that the basis for several different delivery periods can be plotted on the same chart. To assist in developing basis charting, various computer software modeling tools are available. SME brokers can suggest packages that suit individual situations and needs.

Many people ask if the local basis is the same, or similar, from year to year. Similar is more accurate than the same. Thus records of local basis during past years provide a useful starting point when attempting to estimate what the basis may be at various times in the future.

Just as the basis can vary from period to period and from open harvest to closed harvest, it can, and often does, vary from one year to the next. Whenever possible, it is worthwhile to determine why there was a change in the basis compared with previous years. A change from the normal basis level might be permanent or semipermanent. For example, a change may be due to a change in local material demand such as a decline in both new and redesign landscaping projects.

BASIS PREDICTED

Many economic factors can and do influence the basis from period to period. Thus it is obvious that forward basis cannot be predicted exactly.

Example: If a grower hedges Japanese laceleaf maples by selling at a forward price of $365 per tree in anticipation that the basis at the time of delivery will be $25, the basis may or may not turn out to be exactly $25. It may be $20 (thereby netting the grower a higher price than anticipated), or it may be $30 (thereby netting the grower a lower price than anticipated).

The uncertainty of what the basis will be in the future is known as basis risk. Because of basis risk, the results of hedging are not perfect. Even so, basis can generally be predicted with far greater accuracy than the level of prices can. Hedgers are thus able to accept the relatively small risk of an unfavorable basis change and eliminate the larger risk of an unfavorable price-level change.

BASIS AND CASH PRICES

Basis Helps When Making Cash Marketing Decisions

Basis can, and should, be one consideration for cash market pricing. For example, assume that a bid for an April 1994 call for Japanese laceleaf maples is $185 per tree. Noting that the October 1994 forward price is currently quoted at $245, growers can quickly calculate that the bidder is offering to buy their trees at a basis of $60 under the nearby forward. From past experience and records of basis in previous years, growers know that the usual basis in their area has averaged only $40 (which would mean a net price $20 higher than what the bidder is now offering).

There may, of course, be any number of possible reasons for weaker-than-normal basis: An unusually large supply may be causing Japanese laceleaf maples to sell at a greater-than-normal discount relative to forward prices. Or, in the absence of local buyers, growers may be considering bids from more distant locations. Depending on the reasons for the weaker-than-normal basis, growers may want to shop around for a possibly higher price.

On the other hand, if growers believe that a weak basis will prove to be of short duration, they may want to delay selling material in hopes of a more normal basis and a higher selling price. (Bear in mind, however, that any delay in selling runs the risk of a decline in the level of prices.) A $5 improvement in the basis is small consolation if the price level has dropped by $10 or $15 in the meantime.

A Strong Basis Is a Good Time to Sell Material

Typically, a strong basis is an indication that, for some reason or combination of reasons, buyers are currently willing to pay a higher-than-usual price (in relation to forward prices) for material for immediate delivery. This situation may be nationwide, or it may occur only in a limited area.

6

Forward Market Hedging

HEDGING AND ITS PURPOSE

Forward markets exist primarily for hedging, which is defined as the management of price risks inherent in the ownership of commodities. Given the movements between cash and forward market prices, however, speculating can be considered a profitable strategy.

The word *hedge* means protection. *Webster's New World Dictionary* states that to hedge is "to try to avoid or lessen loss . . . by making counterbalancing . . . investments." In the context of forward market trading, that is precisely what a hedge is: A counterbalancing in the forward market that is opposite one's position in the cash commodity. In this manner, any loss in the cash market will be mediated by a gain in the forward market.

Hedgers include:

Growers need protection against declining prices for crops still in the field or in storage. Growers look to secure sales in later years. (Growers also benefit from increased market coverage for their material.)

Wholesalers and rewholesalers need protection against increasing material costs or against decreasing inventory values.

Landscape contractors and landscape architects need protection against higher prices for material needed for future projects or to ensure material availability at the time of need. The use of hedging will also reduce the costs of maintaining inventories.

Garden centers need protection against increasing material costs or to ensure material availability at the time of need.

Landscape brokers need protection against higher prices for materials that they have commitments to sell. They may also desire a more effective way to control material availability.

General contractors need to secure forward prices and supply guarantees for future construction projects on which they are currently bidding.

The primary purpose of hedging is to limit the impact of adverse price-level changes. A hedge is a sale (or purchase) on the forward market for the purpose of establishing a price in advance of actual cash delivery.

For buyers of material, options on forward contracts are a powerful tool for hedging. By purchasing an option on a forward contract, buyers are essentially setting the maximum price that they will pay for that material. At the time of the need for the actual material, should the cash market price be lower than the price available through the option, the holder will purchase material on the cash market. If the price available with the option and forward contract is lower, the buyer will exercise the option. In either case, the option holder will have successfully hedged against adverse price-level changes.

By making material available, to satisfy the forward contracts and options traded on the Seattle Mercantile Exchange, growers are able to lock in sales of material in advance of actual delivery dates. By locking in a delivery date—and a price—growers can protect themselves against any adverse price changes that may occur before the material is delivered. This protection is the hedge.

Regardless of the purpose for which it is employed, hedging consists of taking a position in the forward market that is opposite to that same person's position in the cash market. Growers of Japanese laceleaf maples, for example, are "long" Japanese laceleaf maples in the cash market. They will make money if the price of Japanese laceleaf maples goes up and they have a customer. If the price goes down and they need to sell, for whatever reason, they will lose or make less money.

To hedge against the possibility of a price decline, growers can offset their position in the cash market by taking a "short" position in the forward market, that is, by placing their material on the forward market and selling it by a forward contract. If the price of Japanese laceleaf maples does decline, the potential loss in the cash market is approximately matched by a gain on the forward market and the revenue received when the options sold on the primary market.

Example: In 1994, a grower wants to lock in a particular price for an April 1995 delivery of Japanese laceleaf maples. The grower, through the underwriter or the exchange, learns that April 1995 Japanese laceleaf maples forward contracts sell at $365 per tree, while the 1994 cash market is $250. Subsequently, there is a weakening in the demand for Japanese laceleaf maples, and the local cash price declines by $20, to $230. This decline has little effect because the grower may have a committed buyer at $365. (Why a buyer would pay $365 per tree is explained in Chapter 7.) By multiplying $20 per tree by 100 trees, the grower just saved $2,000 over the local cash market.

LIFTING A HEDGE

A grower or buyer who has purchased an option to hedge can lift the hedge prior to actual material delivery. For holders, lifting a hedge is done by selling (trading) the option on the secondary market or by not exercising the option and letting it expire. Similarly, a grower can lift a hedge (committed material to the "pool") by buying a matching option in the same series at prevailing prices and letting the option expire.

A forward contract holder can lift his or her hedge by selling the contract on the secondary market at prevailing prices. Conversely, a grower can also buy a forward contract at prevailing prices.

In some circumstances, lifting a hedge might be to a grower's advantage. For example, assume that at harvest the grower placed the material in storage and, to protect against a possible price decline, hedged by placing the material on the forward market. Since then, however, there are indications that prices on the cash market may move sharply higher. To take advantage of the expected higher prices, the grower may decide to lift the hedge and sell the material on the cash market. (The risk in doing so, of course, is that time may prove that the grower was mistaken about the direction of prices.)

In addition to these situations, growers may want to lift a hedge simply because the cash price of the commodity has declined to a level at which the growers are now willing to own it without price protection. Any subsequent increase in the price once the hedge is lifted should then result in a profit (to the extent that the increase exceeds storage costs).

Again, to lift a hedge the grower simply contracts his or her broker; options in the same series, if available, are purchased and the grower lets the options expire. This closing transaction releases the grower from having to make delivery on a forward contract already committed to.

GROWERS, BASIS, AND HEDGING: WHAT IS THE BEST DELIVERY MONTH?

Although the price for one particular forward delivery period is higher than the other—that the October forward price, for example, is higher than that of April—this is not necessarily the most profitable period in which to hedge. To make this decision, the grower needs to take into account not only the various forward prices and the carrying charges and product appreciation they reflect, but also the probable basis. This is yet another way in which basis knowledge can be useful—and, indeed invaluable—in marketing decisions.

In addition, underwriters can be extremely helpful, and it is their role to assist the grower with making the right market decision.

Example: Assume that the April 1995 Japanese laceleaf maple forward price is $250 per tree and the October 1995 forward price is simultaneously $300 per tree. At first look, that appears to be a $50 cost for inventorying until October 1995. But the grower's records indicate, based on history, that the normal basis will be $40 in April 1995 and $50 in October 1995. Thus the forward market offers the grower a net of $210 in April '95 ($250 − $40) and $250 in October '95 ($300 − $50), which is a payment of $40 ($250 − $210) per contract period.

As discussed in Chapter 5, there are a variety of ways to use basis data to make market decisions. Armed with an introduction to the arithmetic of basis and an understanding of its importance in nursery material marketing (particularly in hedging), most growers and other marketers of nursery stock quickly recognize opportunities to employ basis knowledge profitably. Moreover, a knowledge of basis is equally valuable to buyers of such materials, such as landscape contractors and wholesalers, who use the market to hedge against rising prices.

To translate a given forward price into a probable price for making or taking delivery, a knowledge of basis is necessary. An ability to translate forward prices into prices for delivery rapidly is essential for effective hedging, and to decide whether and when to hedge. The more information one has about basis at various times of the year, the better equipped one is to make decisions that turn out to be right decisions.

The importance of basis to hedging makes an understanding of it essential in implementing a hedging strategy. Basis knowledge can help in the overall performance of a hedging or speculating program.

A MARKET FOR SPECULATING

Given the interactions between cash and forward market prices, option value may rise and fall. Accordingly, speculating possibilities are almost endless. Should cash market prices increase above the forward contract's strike price, the option covering the forward contract will increase in value.

When this occurs, and there are a limited number of options offered on the primary market, the secondary market will become active. Those seeking a hedge against increasing prices will be anxious to secure options.

There are many option speculating strategies; although the risk is limited to the option premium, it is best to review all possibilities with a broker before embarking on a speculating program. See Chapter 10 for speculating option strategies.

7

Marketing and Pricing

FORWARD MARKET PERFORMANCE

One of the most important roles of the Seattle Mercantile Exchange is to provide buyers and sellers of commodities, such as growers, wholesalers, retailers, landscape contractors, and landscape architects, with an opportunity to establish prices for future delivery. Individuals and firms who use the forward market for this purpose are able to minimize the risk of adverse price-level changes. Moreover, as an alternative material marketing source, the exchange offers the industry "competitive delivery" of the services and materials that are part of the nursery industry.

FORWARD PRICE DETERMINATION

A forward price is a commodity's expected price at some future time and date. Forward prices can be forecast by using the local cash market price as a component of basis. They can be projected for as many periods as are appropriate for the commodity being analyzed. A forward price thus arrived at becomes a statement of the commodity's value at the present time and under present conditions.

FORWARD PRICE ANALYSIS

Forward price analysis falls into two categories. Fundamental analysis looks at factors that affect supply and demand for material. Technical analysis studies volume and past price trends. Forward prices use methods from both approaches, and are generated by combining the material's cash market price with the basis appropriate for each time period.

For example, a buyer looking to purchase material on the forward market will compare the cost to inventory material with the benefits of not having to inventory. A garden center or landscape contractor will factor in the savings gains from not having to pay the typical mark-ups associated with material purchased on the cash market.

Assume that growers are selling Japanese laceleaf maples on the cash market for $200. After various distribution segments apply mark-ups, the garden center, which is two or in some cases three levels into the distribution cycle, will most likely pay $300 per tree. In addition, the garden center estimates that the cost to inventory a tree, until it is sold, to be $65. Therefore, after mark-ups and inventory costs, not to mention the cost of capital, the garden center will have $365 invested in the tree. Any price on the forward market below $365 would be less than what the garden center would pay had it acquired the plant on the cash market.

Therefore, a forward price is a forecast in that, it reflects what buyers and sellers assume the price to be at a future date based on currently available information. Forward prices thus provide a valuable tool for growers and others who make advance plans concerning production, storage, and marketing.

A forward price can be considered a price prediction because at any given time it reflects the price expectations of both buyers and sellers at the time of delivery. In another sense, however, it cannot be considered a prediction because a forward price is a price prediction subject to change. Forward prices adjust to reflect additional information such as supply and demand as it becomes available.

An improvement in the outlook for residential or commercial construction, for example, could lead to forward prices moving upward. A slackening in demand could lead to lower forward prices. Moreover, a forward price can be affected by the way that buyers and sellers react to it. For example, if forward prices are particularly high or low, growers might react by increasing or decreasing production, thereby changing the price outlook.

There are different forward prices for different contract months. This relationship is referred to as spread. The two principal reasons for spread are (1) the material's relative basis (which includes the cost of storing material from one contract month to another) and (2) any appreciation in the material during that time. The expenses of storage— known as carrying charges—are normally reflected in the forward prices for different delivery periods. They include costs such as water, labor, and fertilizer. Another component of spread is material appreciation that may derive from growth or artistic development.

Example: Suppose that a grower in Oregon is growing Japanese laceleaf maples. After accounting for maintenance, labor, and other expenses, the grower determines that it costs $45 a harvest period to store a Japanese laceleaf maple that is ready for harvest and sale. Also, the Japanese laceleaf maple will increase in value (due to increased height and so forth) by $40 per period. If the forward prices reflected the full charges, the prices for different contract month might look like this:

April 1994	October 1994	April 1995	October 1995	April 1996	October 1996
$195	$280	$365	$450	$535	$620

As a practical matter, however, forward prices for the different contract months do not always reflect full carrying charges and appreciation amounts (basis). The price difference is seldom more than the full actual charge. Month-to-month differences can be, and frequently are, less than a full charge. This cost understating occurs for a variety of reasons, such as the willingness of wholesalers to store material or a particularly strong market demand for material for immediate delivery.

In cases studied, the cost to store material (part of basis) has traditionally been underestimated by various segments of the industry. Wholesalers or retailers attempting to lower next year's acquisition costs by purchasing and storing material for sale next year risk more than the savings they seek. In fact, studies demonstrate that it is a common practice for wholesalers, retailers, and landscape contractors to purchase material on the cash market and attempt to develop it to specimen grade. In doing so, these segments are carrying what is called basis risk, the risk that the actual costs to carry the material may be different than anticipated and the risk that the material may not appreciate as anticipated.

For example, the willingness by Northwest buyers to carry basis risk is the driving factor that leads Northwest growers to seek markets in the eastern United States. An argument can be made that Northwest buyers have no choice but to buy nonmature material and carry basis risk because the price for specimen material sold by Northwest growers is influenced by East Coast markets. SME studies have found that nonmature material is purchased by Northwest buyers because the buyers believe, given the long Northwest growing season, that it pays to carry the costs (basis risk) associated with developing material to specimen grade. When all costs are considered, however, the gains are seldom realized.

A recent SME study demonstrates that the lower production costs of nursery stock, long an advantage for Northwest growers, are now coming into line with East Coast growers. Therefore, eastern growers are now producing and selling more material that would typically be grown and sold by Northwest growers.

It seems that growers in the eastern United States are quickly adjusting to market demands. Although the Northwest has a jump on specimen grade stock, eastern growers, the SME study suggests, will soon catch up in overall production and sales. Interestingly, aside from the advantage of a longer growing season, the Northwest is losing its competitive edge of relatively low labor and land costs compared with the same costs in the East. For years, Northwest growers have produced a reasonably priced product compared with what growers in the East could produce. With value and demand increasing for particular genera and species, however, Eastern growers are now offering their local markets competitively priced products.

The 1992 SME study seems to support that consensus. Of the top 10 producing states, Oregon is fourth. Just 5 years ago, Oregon was third, behind Florida (which does not grow the same type of material). But when you compare Oregon with eastern states in which similar plant species are grown, Oregon ranks eighth as measured by percentage of total production. Washington state, which was 10th 5 years ago, is now 13th. When measured by percentage of production, Washington State is 17th.

Therefore, because Northwest specimen grade growers are losing their competitive advantage for holding and developing specimen grade stock, many may soon be locked out of the Eastern market—a market that represents 70% of Northwest sales. Should this happen, price will become the dominant factor for selling material into the region.

All this creates a very interesting scenario: Northwest growers, in the not too distant future, may be supplying the East with more container and fewer specimen grade stocks. For growers currently supplying containers to the East, the windfall may be tremendous. For specimen growers, however, the Northwest market may soon be their only market.

FORWARD CONTRACT PRICES AND FUTURE DELIVERY

Forward prices are not always higher for more distant delivery periods; that is, they do not always incrementally increase upward. Sometimes, albeit infrequently, they step downward. This latter situation is known as an inverted market. Instead of a normal carrying charge and appreciation amount between delivery periods, there is a negative charge. The market is, in effect, paying owners of nursery material to sell it now instead of storing or developing it to specimen grade. The amount by which prices for nearby contract months are above prices for distant contract months depends entirely on how much buyers are willing to pay for immediate delivery.

The usual reasons for an inverted market are an immediate strong demand or a short supply. For example, in a building boom or a natural disaster, buyers need material delivered immediately and are willing to pay a higher price to get it delivered now. The size of the premium depends on how badly buyers want the material and how reluctant growers are to part with it. Growers' hesitancy to sell may be influenced by an expectation that prices will climb even higher.

An inverted market is most likely at a time of short supply, that is, at a time when the supply is small, or expected to be small, in relation to demand. In this situation, to assure an adequate supply and to avoid possibly higher prices later, buyers may be willing to pay a higher price for material that they do not yet need, storage costs and appreciation notwithstanding.

Forward prices and the relationships between forward prices for different contract months are important to sellers of nursery material. By following forward prices, particularly at the time that marketing decisions are made, and by understanding what they mean, growers are able to make informed decisions about selling material now, harvesting at a later date, or boxing the material for specimen development for a subsequent sale. And if, to hedge against price risks, they are considering selling stored material on the forward market, the relationships between different contract months (the amount of the carrying charge and appreciation) can help to decide in which contract months to hedge.

The most important element for forward pricing is the interaction on the cash market. The current price of material is, essentially, the local cash price. This is the current cash market price that is then used as the starting point for the generation of forward prices. To calculate this current price, an analysis of the local cash market in the region of the material's supply is conducted. If the current demand for material is strong or if the available supply is small, the resulting strong cash market may result in a high current price. Conversely, if the current demand for material is weak or if the available supply is large, the resulting weak cash market may result in low current price.

Given that location affects the cash price for material, differences in location—or more specifically, differences in transportation costs due to location—are certainly major issues that a buyer faces when deciding what to pay for material.

LOCATION CAN AFFECT RETURNS

If all transportation were free or if the cost of transportation were not related to distance or specific handling requirements, then buyers would be willing to pay the same price regardless of location. Difference in price may be influenced by quality or limited storage space, which in turn can motivate a grower to sell. Transportation is not free, however, and the transportation costs are related to distance. Buyers seeking to purchase material take the transportation costs into account when deciding what to bid for one grower's material versus another's.

As a result, growers in some communities are at a disadvantage in terms of location and, therefore, in terms of the price they can charge. They may, for example, be located a considerable distance from an active buying market, or they may lack access to low-cost transportation. In contrast, growers at another location may be able to choose between several markets actively competing for their material. Or, they may have an advantage because of several forms of inexpensive transportation. In some instances, they may have both advantages.

Example: Suppose that an East Cost buyer has a market for beech trees in the $300 price range. After calling around, the buyer determines that it will cost $50 for shipment from Oregon and $75 for shipment from California. Assuming the need for a profit margin of $50 per tree, the buyer can afford to pay up to $200 ($300 − $50 − $50) for Oregon beeches and up to $175 ($300 − $50 − $75) for California beeches. Oregon growers thus have an advantage with regard to transportation costs and, knowing this, can charge a higher local cash price for their material.

Usually, but not always, local cash prices and forward prices move up and down together, but infrequently by exactly the same amount. Major supply and demand developments that affect forward prices generally have a similar impact on local cash prices. Examples would be news that supply is up or down or that new construction is higher or lower than expected. On the other hand, a change in the demand for beech in Washington does not necessarily mean that there will be a corresponding change—or any change at all, for that matter—in the demand for the same beech in Oregon or New York. Moreover, local cash prices are not always less than forward prices. In areas that enjoy a location advantage, cash prices are frequently or even consistently higher than forward prices.

It is even possible that forward prices and the cash price in a particular area to move in opposite directions. Such could be the case, for example, if the overall demand for nursery material was weak (thereby having a depressing effect on forward prices) but demand for material in New York was especially strong. An area with a favorable location in relation to the area of demand could thus enjoy an increase in price, declining forward prices notwithstanding.

Even so, forward prices still provide the best available barometer of changes in supply and demand. As a result, short-term changes in cash and forward prices—up as well as down— tend to occur in concert, but not necessarily penny for penny. The relative predictability of the relationship between cash and forward prices makes hedging possible.

Example: Suppose that a landscape contractor holds a Japanese laceleaf maple option with an exercise price of $200 that was purchased for $20 and a wholesaler holds a forward contract for the same Japanese laceleaf maple that was purchased for $220.

1. If a grower, for whatever reason, decides to offer similar quality and grade Japanese laceleaf maples for $150, both the contractor and wholesaler are in a position to take advantage of this price drop. The contractor simply lets the option expire and purchases the tree for $150, at a net expense of $170 ($150 + $20). The wholesaler also purchases the tree for $150 and simultaneously sells the forward contract for $190 to someone who cannot take advantage of the $150 cash market price. The new buyer would be someone who does not have an immediate need

for the material but who wants to hedge against possible higher prices when the material is needed. The forward contract is still worth more than $150 because it does not expire until some future period—a net expense of $180 ($150 + $220 − $190).

2. If the price for a Japanese laceleaf maples increases to $300, then again both the contractor and wholesaler can take advantage of the increase. The contractor can either exercise the option and take delivery at $200, a net expense of $220 ($200 + $20), or can sell the option on the secondary market for, say, $50, thus realizing a $30 ($50 − $20) profit. The wholesaler can either accept delivery of the Japanese laceleaf maple at a net expense of $220 or sell the contract on the secondary market for, say, $250, thus realizing a $30 ($250 − $220) profit. (The contract is worth more than the $220 face price because a Japanese laceleaf maple is currently selling on the cash market for $300.)

In either of the above scenarios, the contractor, wholesaler, and grower successfully hedged against price increases or decreases.

8

Forecasting Forward Prices

INTRODUCTION TO FORECASTING FORWARD PRICES

Few other business activities are more critical to success than the business of forecasting future prices. Make the correct prediction about price trends and levels and ensure success, but make the wrong prediction—or, even worse, make no prediction at all—and disaster is imminent. From a physician predicting legal and insurance costs to a manufacturer predicting raw material costs and finished goods prices, forecasting occurs in all industries. The ability to make accurate and reliable material price forecasts is becoming increasingly important in the nursery materials industry.

FORWARD CONTRACT PRICING

There is an old story about a seeker of knowledge who searches for the answer to a question that has troubled him for a long time. In his traavels he hears of two very wise men who are said by many to be very knowledgeable and experienced in such matters. The first, a famous guru, lives at the top of a mountain, high above the hustle and bustle of everyday life. After a long and strenuous climb, the seeker poses his question: "What is a forward contract worth?" The guru answers immediately that it is not hard to prove that

$$F_{t,T} = P_t(1 + r_{t,T}) + SC_{t,T} - CV_{t,T}$$

where F is forward price, P is the current cash market price, R is the risk-free interest rate, SC is the future value of storage costs, CV is the future value of convenience values, and T is future time. Of course, this has to be modified somewhat in practice to reflect dividends and a few other technical details.

The answer seems pretty exact, if a bit complicated. The seeker thanks the guru warmly and goes on his way.

The second wise man lives in the middle of a big city, surrounded by a continuous swirl of noise and activity. Once the seeker is able to get his attention, he poses the question again: "What is a forward contract worth?" Again the answer is immediate: "That depends. Are you buying them or selling them?" the wise man asks.

Not knowing quite what to say, the seeker responds by repeating the words and equation of the first guru, but he is quickly interrupted. "I don't care about all that stuff. Tell him to make me a bid. Then we can talk about what a forward contract is really worth," the wise man says. Somewhat confused and not at all sure that the wise men's answers have brought him any closer to enlightenment, the seeker goes to meditate further on his question.

The moral of this story is that theory and analysis can say what a forward contract should be worth, but the interactions of buyers and sellers of forward contracts determine its price. In the ideal market, if a contract's price is less than its worth, arbitrageurs can trade it against the offsetting cash market position to produce a position that is riskless over time but that will provide a higher return than the risk-free profit by exactly the same amount that the contract was overpriced in the first place. To see why this is so, first develop the fundamental no-arbitrage equation.

THE FUNDAMENTAL NO-ARBITRAGE EQUATION

The fundamental no-arbitrage equation states that at all times, the price of a forward contract must equal the sum of its current cash market price, interest costs, and storage costs, less any convenience values. In mathematical notation, for a forward contract delivering at time T, the fundamental no-arbitrage equation for transformable nursery materials with no associated convenience value is

$$F_{now} = P_{now}(1 + r_{now,T}) + SC_{,now,T} - CV_{now,T}$$

where F_{now} is today's forward price of the deliverable grade, P_{now} is today's cash market price of the grade of commodity that will grow to the deliverable grade by time of delivery, $r_{now,t}$ is the interest rate cost from now until time T, $sc_{now,T}$ is the future value of storage costs from today until time T, and $CV_{now,T}$ is any convenience value associated with holding the commodity until time T. Also note that $SC_{now,T}$ is the future value at time T of all the noninterest costs incurred while transforming the commodity to the deliverable grade. These costs can be substantial; they include labor costs, agricultural chemical costs, and crop insurance. The use of the fundamental no-arbitrage equation is demonstrated in the following example.

Example: Suppose that today you notice that a buyer in the market is willing to pay $400 for a forward contract delivering 1 ounce of gold exactly 6 months from now. At the same time, you notice that gold is currently selling in the cash market for $340 per ounce. Telephone calls net you the following information: Your bank will lend you money at a 6-month interest cost of 5%, a safe deposit box can be rented for 6 months for $15, and you see no convenience value associated with holding gold for that period.

Many will already realize that there is an opportunity for riskless profit here through the use of arbitrage. To take advantage of this opportunity, the procedure is as follows:

1. Borrow $355 ($340 + $15) from the bank at 5%, purchase 1 ounce of gold on the cash market (and place it in the newly rented safe deposit box), and sell the buyer one 6-month forward contract for $400. Notice that as of this time you have neither spent nor received any of your own money; you will not receive the $400 until the forward contract expires in 6 months. The net cash flow is zero ($355 − $340 − $15).

2. Six months from now you deliver the gold into the forward contract, use the proceeds to pay off the bank, and walk away with a risk-free profit of $27! This was calculated as follows:

$400	Proceeds from forward contract
− $355	Principal of loan
− $18	Interest due on loan (355 × 5%)
$27	

How did this happen? In this case, the forward market was overpriced relative to the cash market and associated carrying costs. Thus an arbitrageur (you in the above example) can replicate the forward contract using real assets (gold, safe deposit box for storage, and so on) at a lower cost and then sell on the overpriced markets (forward contracts) and buy on the underpriced market (cash market). In doing so, the arbitrageur nets the difference between the two prices.

In the real world, this opportunity would not exist, and even if it did, it would not last long. Many individuals would seek to sell forward contracts at $400, causing an excess supply of forward contracts, which would cause the price to fall. At the same time, many individuals would seek to buy gold on the cash market, causing an excess demand for gold, which would cause the price to rise. The combination of these selling and buying pressures would drive the prices into equilibrium, which is exactly what the fundamental no-arbitrage equation states: The price in the forward market must be in equilibrium with (equal to) the cash market price and associated carrying costs.

CONVENIENCE VALUE

Before discussing convenience value associated with nursery materials, it is necessary to understand the difference between a pure asset and a convenience asset. A pure asset is an asset held only for its expected capital gains and explicit payouts. Stocks and bonds are pure assets. A convenience asset is held only by those who receive a benefit in addition to the expected capital gains and explicit payouts. Commodities are frequently held as convenience assets.

For example, consider the reasons for holding corn. Corn prices tend to rise before a harvest (as supply shrinks) and fall after a harvest (as supply grows). An investor who buys corn just before a harvest and holds it until just after will most likely suffer a capital loss. Further, that investor must pay for storage costs and will receive no pay outs. Thus investors are unlikely to hold corn through a harvest for pure investment purposes. They may, however, hold it for other reasons. A corn processor, for example, might hold corn to avoid having to close the plant in the event of a temporary corn shortage. The value of such potential uses of corn is called convenience value. If the corn processor had certain knowledge that there would not be a shortfall, however, there would receive no convenience value; the corn processor would then have no reason to hold the corn over the harvest period.

In the example about buying gold, the subject of convenience value was largely avoided by assuming that it was zero. Convenience value is also referred to as a full-carry market because investors are willing to hold the underlying asset for pure investment purposes. The forward price thus reflects the full observable net carry cost for the asset. A non–full-carry market has a positive convenience value because investors are holding the underlying asset for some convenience purposes. The forward price does not reflect the full observable net carry cost for the asset. But is there convenience value associated with nursery material forward contracts?

To answer this question, we look for seasonal patterns in a model of nursery material production and usage. The model is for a world with no uncertainty; in other words, in this scenario, all production and usage is known with certainty.

Suppose that the material harvest begins in late October and runs through early April of the following year and that material is used at a constant rate throughout the year. Also suppose that there is no uncertainty about the harvest size or the usage rate. Figure 8.1 graphs the production and usage patterns over several years. Figure 8.2 shows what happens to material inventories under these patterns. When production exceeds usage, inventories increase, and when usage outpaces production, inventories fall. Inventories reach zero just when production begins to exceed usage at the start of the harvest period.

Because there is no convenience value in a world of certainty, the only storage will be for pure investment purposes. In this model, material is a pure asset when it is stored between harvests. Therefore, the material's cash price must rise between harvests at a rate that covers both interest and physical storage costs. This price rise is shown in Figure 8.3. When inventories reach zero during the next harvest, material is no longer a pure asset and the price does not have to rise to cover interest and storage costs.

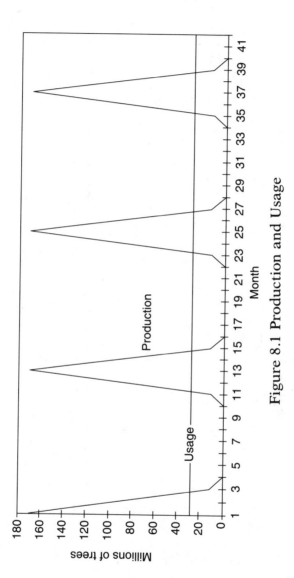

Figure 8.1 Production and Usage

113

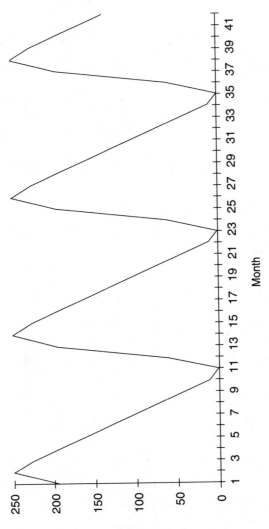

Figure 8.2 Inventories

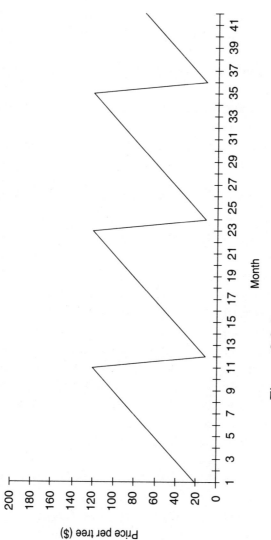

Figure 8.3 Spot Market Price

In fact, the price will fall back to the previous harvest's level because supply and demand at harvest are identical every year. This pattern will repeat over time, as Figure 8.3 demonstrates.

In the real world, the nursery materials market is loaded with uncertainties. Weather patterns affect material growth rates, harvest sizes, and material survival rates. Harvesting decisions are not generally known. Furthermore, demand for material depends on the overall health of the economy. Yet many of the certainty model's inventory and cash price characteristics still hold in the actual world of uncertainty. Actual inventories are lowest in late summer and early fall, just prior to the start of the harvest period. They peak in late winter and early spring as harvest is completed. They then decline as usage outpaces production.

Material prices in the real world also behave much like the prices in the certainty case. The lowest prices frequently occur in winter and early spring during the harvest. The highest prices are more spread out, although they almost never occur during the harvest. Despite the great uncertainty in the material markets, this pattern is similar to that of the certainty case in which material prices reach their lowest level at harvest.

The actual material market, however, does not completely conform to the patterns shown in the certainty model. In the real world, there is considerable material storage over harvests, which the certainty model does not predict. The certainty model suggests that no one will hold inventories if prices are expected to drop, as they do during a harvest.

There are two explanations for this material storage over the harvest period. The first is attributed to overharvesting of material. Because there is a limited time when material can be harvested, growers must make their sales volume forecasts well in advance of actual material sales.

To avoid running out of material late in the summer, when prices are actually the firmest, growers will deliberately harvest more nursery material than required. This overstocking is possible because unsold material is not a total write-off. It is usually cost-effective for growers to maintain the overstocked material (in containers, for example), allow it to continue to grow and to appreciate in value, and then sell at a later date.

In essence, growers are executing an investment strategy comparable with that of a pure asset. The growers are not seeking convenience value for storing material over the harvest period.

A second reason for inventory storage is found further down the distribution chain from the grower. Nursery material wholesalers, rewholesalers, and others may purchase material without anticipating immediate sale because they believe that it is cost-effective for them to develop the material to a higher grade. Typically, this strategy is not wise, however, because it is unusual for a wholesaler to be as cost-effective in developing material to the higher grades as a grower.

This analysis suggests that although nursery materials are not clearly pure or convenience assets, their price and inventory data are more characteristic of a pure asset. Some of the nursery material in inventory is not receiving convenience value. Thus convenience value is less important to the determination of forward prices than interest and storage costs, and the nursery material markets are likely to be at full carry.

TRANSFORMABLE COMMODITIES

Nursery material forward contracts differ from the more familiar grain forward contracts in that the underlying assets of the forward contracts are transformable commodities, commodities that grow and change over time. With contracts on soybeans, corn, or even gold, a commodity that is deliverable today can be bought today and can be delivered in the future. For example, if an investor buys 10,000 bushels of soybeans today, the same soybeans will be deliverable into a forward contract 6 months from now.

In contrast, if 5,000 black pines are bought today, the same pines will increase in size (and value) over the intervening 6 months and will be suitable for delivery into a contract for a higher grade of material. If the desire is to deliver pines into a forward contract 6 months from now, smaller pines that will grow to the deliverable grade over the intervening 6 months must be purchased. Over time, the pines will transform into the deliverable grade.

Nursery material markets are likely to be at full carry because some material in inventory will receive no convenience value. Due to the high costs of transacting in these markets, most nursery material arbitrage is likely to be quasiarbitrage. If the forward price is too high relative to the cash market, growers will add to their stocks or refrain from selling from them. If the forward price is too low relative to the spot, they will sell off some of their stock or refrain from harvesting more. These actions will enforce the fundamental no-arbitrage price.

Figures 8.4 through 8.14 show typical growth patterns of the commodities currently being traded on the Seattle Mercantile Exchange.

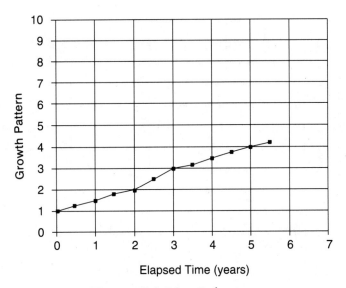

Figure 8.4 *Acer Palmatum*

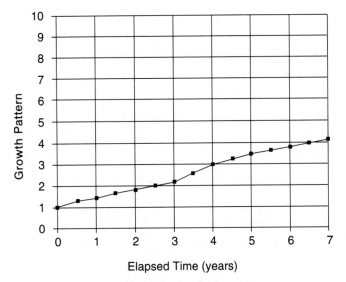

Figure 8.5 *Acer Palmatum Atropurpureum*

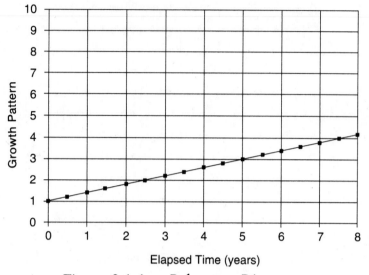

Figure 8.6 *Acer Palmatum Dissectum*

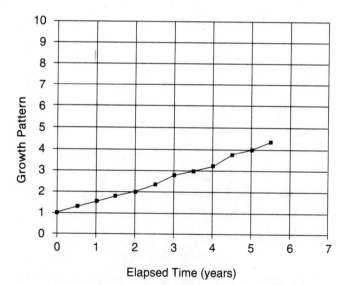

Figure 8.7 *Cercidiphyllum Japonicum*

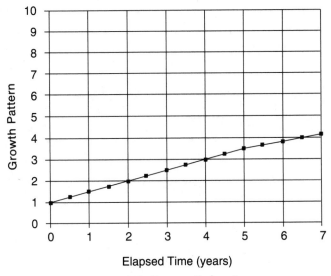

Figure 8.8 *Fagus Sylvatica*

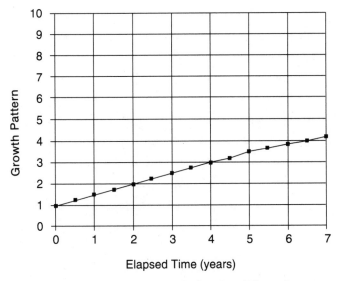

Figure 8.9 *Fagus Sylvatica Riversi*

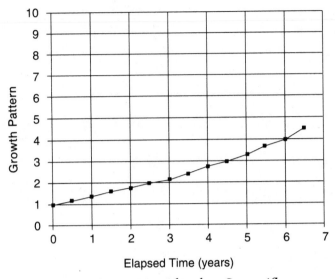

Elapsed Time (years)

Figure 8.10 *Liquidambar Styraciflua*

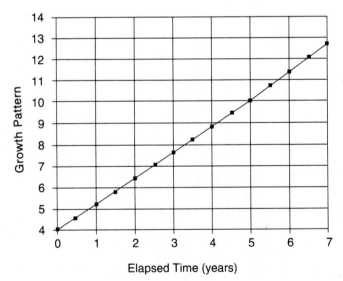

Elapsed Time (years)

Figure 8.11 *Picea Pungens*

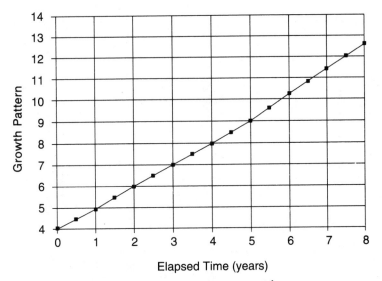

Figure 8.12 *Picea Pungens Glauca*

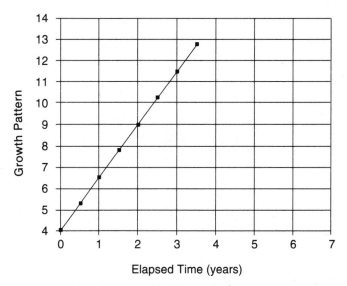

Figure 8.13 *Pinus Sylvestris*

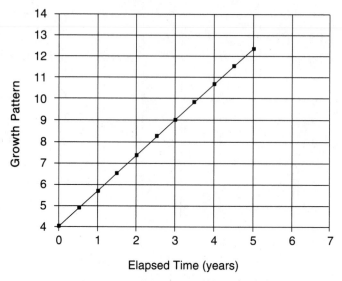

Growth Pattern

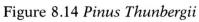

Elapsed Time (years)

Figure 8.14 *Pinus Thunbergii*

9

Primary Option Pricing

HOW THE OPTION PREMIUM IS SET

A knowledge of forward pricing, discussed in Chapter 8, helps in understanding the dynamics of forward contract to cash market pricing. Establishing the option premium should now make sense.

Option buyers pay a price for the right to buy an underlying forward contract (SME forward contracts consist of 25 trees.) This price is called the option premium. The premium is paid to the writer, or seller, of an option. In return, the writer of a call option is obligated to deliver the underlying forward contract in return for the strike price per tree (strike or exercise price is the price set per tree) to an option buyer if the call is exercised; likewise, the writer of a put option is obligated to take delivery of the underlying forward contract (at a cost of the strike price per tree) from an option buyer if the put is exercised. Regardless of an option ever being exercised, the writer keeps the premium. Premiums are quoted on a per tree basis. Thus a premium of 4 represents a premium payment of $100 per option contract ($4 × 25 trees).

Before discussing option premium pricing, it is important to realize that options act as price equalizers. In a forward market, an ideal situation exists when the cash market and forward market prices are identical on the day an option is exercised to a forward contract. This is commonly referred to as convergence. One of the many functions that options have in a forward market is to facilitate the convergence of forward market and cash market prices.

Should the cash market be above the option's strike price, the option's price will increase to satisfy the disparity between the cash market and forward market prices (that is, it will decrease to adjust for disparity).

From the time the option is introduced on the primary market to its expiration date, cash market prices may rise and fall, above or below, forward market prices. Any movement of prices on the cash market will have a direct impact on an option's price (value). Option pricing, therefore, works as a price equilibrium to balance the cash market to forward market prices. This equilibrium is accomplished by the market bidding the option up or down so that the option's underlying strike price, when including the price of the option, is closer at the time of exercise to the nursery material's cash market price.

Example: The strike price of an option's underlying forward contract is $200 per tree. The cash market price is $250. The option will be bid up (or down) to reflect the $50 disparity. Therefore, forward market to cash market convergence is assisted by the option (strike price of $200 + option at $50 = cash market price of $250 (see Table 9.1). All things being equal, if the cash market were $240, the option would most likely trade to $40, and so on. As the option's contract month nears and the market seeks convergence, option prices will constantly change. Given this convergence interaction, options may be traded many times prior to the option's expiration date; hence there is the market for hedging and speculating.

TABLE 9.1
OPTION EQUILIBRIUM—CASH TO FORWARD MARKET PRICE CONVERGENCE

	February	March	April	
Forward contract strike price			200 ⌉	
Cash market price	220	240	250	Equals cash market
Option premium	20	40	50 ⌋	

OPTION PRICING AND FORWARD CONTRACTS

Several factors, as just discussed, contribute value to an option contract and thereby influence the premium at which it is traded. The most important factors are the price of the underlying forward contract, the time remaining until expiration, and the volatility of the nursery material on the cash market.

To make option pricing easier to understand, we will approach this section in three parts. Part 1 focuses on what, if anything, a particular option will be worth at expiration (the last day it is traded). Part 2 deals with how premiums are calculated at issuance and day to day during the time prior to expiration. Part 3 covers some additional, and no less important, contributors to option value.

Part 1: What A Given Option Is Worth At Expiration

An option's value at expiration will reflect whatever amount of money the option holder could realize by exercising the option. If no money could be realized, the option would have no value; it would clearly expire worthless. To understand this more clearly, there are some terms you should know:

Intrinsic value: The amount that an option is in the money is called intrinsic value. This is the amount of money that could be currently realized by exercising an option with a given strike price. A call option has intrinsic value if its strike price is below the material's cash market price for the given delivery period.

Example: Suppose that in June 1995, an October 1995 call option with a forward contract strike price of $500 (October

1995 500 call) was purchased. It is currently September 1995, and the price on the cash market for the same period has risen to $600. Because of this price increase, the call option has an intrinsic value of $100 ($600 − $500).

In the money: In the jargon of options trading, an option, whether a call or put, that has intrinsic value (that is, one that would be worthwhile to exercise) is said to be in the money by the amount of its intrinsic value. At expiration, the value of a given option will be whatever amount, if any, that the option is in the money.

Example: Assume that a $30 premium was paid for a call option with a forward contract strike price of $400, and the cash market price at the option's expiration date has since risen to $450. By how much is the option in the money? The option is in the money by $50 ($450 − $400). The premium is not used in calculating the amount that the option is in the money.

Out of the money: A call option is said to be out of the money if the cash market price is currently below the option's strike price. A put option is out of the money if the cash market price is above the option's strike price.

At the money: If an option strike price and the cash market price are the same, the option is at the money. Even so, an option that is at the money will still have no intrinsic value (it may not be worthwhile to exercise) and, like an out-of-the-money option, is left to expire worthless.

In summary, if, at expiration, an option is not worth exercising, it will expire worthless.

Example: Assume that a $40 premium was paid for a call option with a forward contract strike price of $300, and the cash market price at the option's expiration date has since risen to $350. What is the option's intrinsic value? With the cash market price at $350, a call with a strike price of $300 would have an intrinsic value of $50 ($350 − $300).

Example: Assume the same facts as above, except that at expiration the cash price has fallen to $250. What is the option's intrinsic value? If the cash price at expiration is $250, a call conveying the right to purchase the forward contract at $300 would be worthless $300 > $250), and the option would expire unexercised.

Part 2: How Premiums Are Calculated

If an investor has bought an option and wants to sell it prior to expiration, how much will that person be able to get for it? Its intrinsic value, if any, is already known. But how are option premiums determined? Will an investor have to pay $30 for a particular option, or will it cost $10? $15? If someone wants to sell an option that has not yet expired, will he or she be able to get $20, $30, $40, or what?

In a marketplace, where there is competition between buyers seeking to pay the lowest possible premium and sellers seeking to earn the highest possible premium, there is obviously no set formula for determining what the premium will be for any option at any given time. Option premiums, like the forward prices of the underlying forward contracts, are determined by supply and demand. But remember, option premiums are also governed by cash and forward market prices.

Supply and demand analysis ratios, grower costs, opportunity costs, and so forth are all factored into the development of a forward price. The forward market has definite financial advantages over the cash market for the sale and purchase of nursery material, and it attempts to reflect those advantages in the material's pricing structure by distributing those advantages equally to buyer and seller. Therefore, once the market has calculated their advantages, a price that the market is willing to pay or accept for nursery material is the main component to establishing an option premium.

Part 3: Additional Contributions to Option Value

The option's value to the option holder, which can only be calculated by the holder, must consider three additional elements:

1. The savings of not having to inventory material purchased on the cash market but still having the same control (in typical cases, a savings of $75 to $85 per year per tree)
2. The value of not having to tie up capital for inventory
3. The value of knowing that the material is a telephone call away

These three elements, especially the avoidance of inventory costs, significantly influence the value of an option to its holder.

Example: Assume that a 1-year call option has a forward contract strike price of $400, and the cash market price at the option's expiration date is estimated to be $300. What is this option worth? The option is out of the money, and its intrinsic value is zero ($300 < $400). The option has no time value because there is no possibility of the cash market price rising above the $400 forward market level. In terms of controlling material, however, the option still has value to its holder. To control similar material without the option would require purchasing material on the cash market and then paying for its storage at a typical rate of $75 per tree per year. By purchasing the option, the $75 to control the material is avoided and the acquisition costs are reduced. The cost of capital—or for that matter, the need to tie up capital—is also avoided.

INTRINSIC VALUE AND TIME VALUE

It can be said that option premiums consist of two components, intrinsic value and time value. An option's premium at any given time is the total of its intrinsic value and time value:

Intrinsic value + time value = premium

To recap, the intrinsic value of an option's premium is the amount by which an option is currently in the money. For a call, it is the amount by which the cash market price is above the option's strike price. For a put, it is the amount by which the cash market price is below the strike price.

If an option were out of the money or at the money, the option would have no intrinsic value; its intrinsic value would be zero. The premium would consist solely of time value and avoidable costs value. Stated simply, time value is equal to the premium less the intrinsic value. It is governed by the time remaining to expiration.

Example: Suppose that in August 1994 a Japanese laceleaf maple April 1995 250 call was purchased. In October 1994 the cash market revises downward and Japanese laceleaf maple in April 1995 can be purchased for $230. The option is out of the money ($250 > $230) and has no intrinsic value. Even so, the option is not worthless, because the option still has time to go before it expires, and, during that time, the investor hopes that the April 1995 cash market price will rise above the $250 strike price. Suppose that a buyer is willing to pay a premium of $12 to purchase the option. If the April 1995 cash market price were to climb above $262 (strike price of $250 plus the premium of $12), the new holder of the option would realize a profit.

At this point it should be apparent why an option's premium at expiration will consist only of intrinsic value. Such an option would no longer have time value, for the simple reason that there is no longer any time remaining.

Now return to the out-of-the-money call, which commanded a time value premium of $12 per tree. The next question is, Why $12? Why not $10? Or $20? In other words, what factors influence an option's time value? There are two primary factors: the length of time remaining until expiration and the volatility of the underlying forward prices.

Length of Time Remaining until Expiration

All else remaining equal, the more time an option has until expiration, the higher its premium. This is because it has more time to increase in value (to employ an analogy, it is safer to bet that it will rain within the next 5 days than to bet that it will rain within the next 2 days). Again assuming that all else remains the same, an option's time value will decline (erode) as the option approaches expiration. Thus options are sometimes described as wasting assets. An option at expiration will have no time value; its only value, if any, will be its intrinsic value.

Volatility of the Underlying Forward Prices

All else remaining the same, option premiums are higher during periods of volatile cash market prices. There is more price risk involved in volatile markets and, therefore, a greater need for price protection. The cost of obtaining the price insurance associated with options is greater, and thus the premiums will be higher, than in steady markets. Given that an option will increase in value when cash market prices are more volatile, buyers will be willing to pay more for the option. And because an option is more likely to become worthwhile to exercise when prices are volatile, sellers become less willing to write options and require higher premiums at that time.

Thus an option with 6 months to expiration may command a higher premium in a volatile market than an option with 8 months to expiration in a stable market. Option premiums, therefore, are influenced by the relationship between cash market prices and the option strike price. All else being equal (such as volatility and length of time to expiration), an at-the-money option will have more time value than an out-of-the-money option, because the at-the-money call stands a much better chance of eventually becoming worthwhile to exercise.

It may be surprising to learn that an at-the-money option is likely to have more time value than an option that is substantially in the money, referred to as a deep in-the-money option. One attraction of trading options is leverage, the ability to control relatively large resources with a relatively small investment. An option will not trade for less than its intrinsic value, so when an option is in the money, buyers generally have to pay over and above the option's intrinsic value for the option rights. A deeper in-the-money option requires a greater investment and compromises the leverage associated with the option. Therefore, the time value of the option erodes.

Generally speaking, for a given time to expiration, the greater an option's intrinsic value, the less time value it is likely to have. At some point, a deep in-the-money option may have no time value, even though there is still time remaining until expiration.

PRICING SUMMARY

In the final analysis, the three most important things to know about option premium determination are as follows:

1. Premiums are determined by supply and demand, through competition between buyers and sellers.

2. At expiration, an option will have only intrinsic value (the amount that can be realized by exercising the option). If an option has no intrinsic value at expiration, it will expire worthless. At expiration, an option has no further time value.

3. Prior to expiration, an option's premium will consist of its intrinsic value, if any, plus its time value, if any. If an option has no intrinsic value, its premium prior to expiration will be simply its time value.

CASE STUDY: OPTION PREMIUM DETERMINATION

This case study focuses primarily on the interactions of intrinsic and time value. As mentioned earlier, options also offer value through reductions in inventory, capital, and certainty costs.

At the start of 1994, a 2-year call option is available on a forward contract for Japanese laceleaf maples with the following list of forward prices. These forward prices are thus the strike prices for the call option:

Year	Month	Future Cash Prices	Option Strike Prices
1994	April	$200	$200
	October	$250	$250
1995	April	$300	$300
	October	$350	$350

At the time of issuance, the cash market price for a Japanese laceleaf maple of this grade and size is $200 per tree.

The option's premium is determined as follows:

1. The intrinsic value is zero because the strike prices are the same as the future cash prices for all periods.

2. The time value is nonzero because the option has 2 years until expiration. After evaluating the potential volatility of the Japanese laceleaf maple market over these 2 years, the time value is calculated to be, say, $30.

At the start of April 1994, the option's premium is

$$\text{Premium} = \$0 + \$30 = \$30$$

Now consider a revised forecast for October 1994 cash market prices. Because of an upturn in the economy, demand for materials is high and prices have risen. (The option strike prices are the same prices shown above and are listed here for easy reference.)

Year	Month	Future Cash Prices	Option Strike Prices
1994	October	$270	$250
1995	April	$320	$300
	October	$370	$350

The cash market price for a Japanese laceleaf maple has risen to $270.

The option's premium is determined as follows:

1. **The** intrinsic value is $20 because the cash market prices have risen $20 higher than the strike prices available through the option.
2. **The** time value is still nonzero because the option has 1½ years until expiration. The market currently values this duration at, say, $25.

Thus the October 1994 option's premium is

$$\text{Premium} = \$20 + \$25 = \$45$$

The April 1994 forecast of cash market prices is as follows. Material demand is similar to the last period, and prices are steady. (The option strike prices are the same prices shown above and are listed here for easy reference.)

Year	Month	Future Cash Prices	Option Strike Prices
1995	April	$320	$300
	October	$370	$350

The cash market price for a Japanese laceleaf maple has held steady at $320.

The option's premium is determined as follows:

1. **The** intrinsic value is still $20 because the cash market prices have remained $20 higher than the strike prices available through the option.
2. **The** time value is still nonzero because the option has 1 year until expiration. The market currently

138

values this duration at say, $18. The April 1995 option's premium is

$$\text{Premium} = \$20 + \$18 = \$38$$

In October 1995, the month this call option expires, a forecast of cash market prices is as follows. Because of an economic downturn, demand for material is sluggish and prices have fallen. (The option strike prices are the same prices shown above and are listed here for easy reference.)

Year	Month	Cash Prices	Option Strike Prices
1995	October	$340	$350

The cash market price for a Japanese laceleaf maple has slipped to $340.

The option's premium is determined as follows:

1. The intrinsic value is now zero because the cash market price is lower than the strike price available through the option ($340 < $350). In other words, it is less expensive to purchase a Japanese laceleaf maple on the cash market than it is to purchase it by exercising the option.

2. The time value is still nonzero because the option has 6 months until expiration. The market currently values this duration at, say, $10. Buyers are willing to pay $10 in the hope that the price for a Japanese laceleaf maple will rise enough for them to make a profit (that is, the price must rise above $360, which is the $350 strike price plus the $10 premium). This price rise could only happen if the cash market price rises.

In October 1995 the option's premium would be

$$Premium = \$0 + \$10 = \$10$$

Assuming that the cash market price remains at \$340, then prior to October 1995 the option's premium would gradually fall to 0 as the time value erodes. At the time of expiration the option's premium would consist only of its intrinsic value, which, in this case is 0 because the strike price is higher than the cash market price.

OTHER PRICING FACTORS

Time Remaining until Expiration

Generally, the longer the time remaining until an option's expiration date, the higher the option premium because of the greater possibility that the underlying cash market price might move so as to make the option in the money. The time value premium drops rapidly in the last several weeks of an option's life.

Volatility

Volatility is the propensity of the underlying cash market price to fluctuate, either up or down. This volatility influences the option premium. The higher the volatility, the higher the premium because of the greater possibility that the option will move in the money.

OPTION PRICING MODELS

It was shown earlier that the pricing of forward contracts is governed by arbitrage, with buyers and sellers attempting to profit on discrepancies between the cash and forward market prices. Option prices on the primary market as well as the secondary market are also governed by arbitrage. The trading strategies used in arbitrage in the options markets are significantly more complicated than those of the forward contract and cash markets. This section uses a greatly simplified example to help develop an intuitive understanding of how options are priced. The next section examines one of the most widely used option pricing models in existence, the Black and Scholes option pricing model.

Two-State Pricing

Similar to forward contract pricing, where the cash market price, interest rates, and carrying costs helped to dictate the fundamental no-arbitrage forward price, option prices are also governed by equivalent investment prices. Investment strategies with identical profit-and-loss performance should cost exactly the same to implement. Suppose, for example, that Secure Bank was selling a 1-year certificate of deposit (CD) for $900. This CD will pay, to the holder, $1000 in 1 year, giving a $100 profit to the holder. Right next door to Secure Bank is Safe Bank (of identical reputation and security), which is selling a 1-year certificate of deposit that will pay, to its holder, $2,000 in 1 year. The price of this CD *must* be, at most, $1,800 (giving a $200 profit to the holder).

Why? If the second CD were priced at, say, $1,850, potential investors could earn more money simply by buying two of the $900 CDs (see Table 9.2). Safe Bank would be unable to sell its CDs and would be forced to lower its asking price.

What would happen if Safe Bank sold its CD for less than $1,800? Then the opposite would be true. In that case, investors could earn more from the Safe Bank CD, and no

TABLE 9.2
SECURE BANK AND SAFE BANK CD PRICING

Initial Investment		Payoff	Profit	Yield
Buy one CD:				
Secure Bank	$900	$1,000	$100	11%
Safe Bank	$1,850	$2,000	$150	8%
Buy two CDs:				
Secure Bank	$900	$1,000	$100	11%
	$900	$1,000	$100	11%
	$1,800	$2,000	$200	11%

one would buy the Secure Bank CD. Secure Bank would be forced to lower its price. (In this example we assume that potential investors have at least $1,800 to invest and are not constrained by having to invest more than $900.)

The price of an option is determined in a very similar way. First, the price of another, equivalent investment strategy is found. The price of the option must be the same as the price of this strategy.

To illustrate, assume that the current price of a select variety of Japanese laceleaf maple is $340 per tree and that this price will change only once during the coming year. Further, assume that the price of this Japanese laceleaf maple 1 year from now will be either $405 or $310 per tree. Last, assume that the interest rate at which money can be borrowed or lent is 9%. We wish to determine the price of a 1-year call option on one Japanese laceleaf maple under these conditions.

Here are two potential investment strategies that can be used:

Strategy 1: Purchase two 1-year call options with strike prices of $357.50 per tree. Because the premium for these options is not known now, refer to it as $C.

Strategy 2: Buy one tree for $340 and partially finance the purchase by borrowing $285 for 1 year.

The profit and loss performance of these two strategies is shown in Table 9.3. We can see that even though strategy 2 does not involve using options, it gives (in this model) exactly the same payoff as strategy 1. There is no profit if the price of a Japanese laceleaf maple falls to $310, and a $95 profit if the price rises to $405. Thus we can create what is called a synthetic call option by following strategy 2. In this example we must hold one tree for every two options we wish to replicate.

The number of trees needed to duplicate the option is called the option's delta (Δ), which factors into the price of an option.

The equivalence of the two investment strategies allows an investor to calculate the price for a single call option. Strategy 2 gives $95 in profit for a cost of $55. Strategy 1 also gives $95 in profit for a cost of $2C. Because the profit/loss performance is identical, the cost for each strategy must be identical. Thus strategy 1 must cost $55, or $55/2 = $27.50 per call option. If call options sold for any other price, an arbitrage opportunity would exist and buyers and sellers would move to make profits. Their activities would quickly drive the option prices to their fundamental no-arbitrage level of $27.50 per option.

This simple example allows us to derive the following formula:

$$\text{Call option price} = \Delta \times \text{share} - \text{borrowing}$$

where share refers to gold, stock, or other underlying asset (in this case, trees).

Observe what information is necessary to derive the price of the call option: the current cash market price, the option's strike price, the option's expiration date, the

TABLE 9.3
PROFIT-AND-LOSS PERFORMANCE OF STRATEGIES 1 AND 2

Strategy	Cost	Price = $130	Price = $405
1: Buy two calls	$2C	$2 \times 0 = 0$	$2 \times \$47.50 = \$ 95$
2: Buy one tree	$340	$310	$405
Borrow	$285	$285 \times 1.09 = \$310$	$285 \times 1.09 = 405$
Total	$340 - \$285 = \$55$	$310 - \$310 = 0$	$405 - \$405 = 0$

riskless interest rate, and the possible cash prices at time of expiration. But perhaps more significant is what information is *not* required to determine the option's price. A call option makes money if the cash market price of the underlying asset rises; it loses money if this cash market price falls. Thus one would quickly conclude that the price of the option is governed by the relative probabilities of price increases and decreases. This conclusion would be wrong.

The option payoff for both Japanese laceleaf maple price increases and decreases can be replicated with the synthetic strategy. Two arbitrageurs might disagree on the relative probabilities that the cash market price of a Japanese laceleaf maple will rise or fall, but they cannot disagree on the price of the option. Also not needed are risk-adjusted interest rates. One might believe that because options are risky assets, then risk-adjusted discount rates to price them are needed. Again, this conclusion would be in error. Our pricing strategy requires only the riskless rate of interest.

BLACK AND SCHOLES'S FORMULA

In 1973 two financial theorists from the University of Chicago, Fischer Black and Myron Scholes, published a revolutionary paper showing that when the prices of an option's underlying commodity (gold, stock, and so forth) shift continuously, as they do in the real world, the pricing intuition presented earlier still holds. In 1976 Black showed that this logic was also applicable to the pricing of futures (forward) contracts.

It was demonstrated that a synthetic call option can be created by buying a delta share of the underlying asset and borrowing to finance some of the purchase. The portion of the purchase cost not covered by borrowing is the cost of replicating the option. As stated, arbitrageurs help ensure that the market price of a call option is identical to that of its replicating strategy, or portfolio. Black and Scholes showed that when stock prices move continuously, one can still replicate the option by following a strategy of buying (going long) delta shares of the underlying asset and borrowing to finance a portion of the purchase. They proved that

$$\text{Replicating portfolio cost} = \text{current share price} \times \text{number of shares} - \text{borrowing}$$
$$= \text{current share price} \times \Delta - \text{borrowing}$$

Black showed that call options on futures can be priced using similar strategies to construct replicating portfolios. These strategies involve going long delta futures for each call to be replicated, including borrowing. Therefore, the logic to construct replicating portfolios is exactly the same. The profit or loss performance of a call option on a futures contract can be replicated with combinations of buying futures and borrowing, and thus the option prices are governed by arbitrage.

For the mathematically inclined reader, Black's formula for call options on futures is presented next.

The cost of the replicating portfolio for a call option on a futures contract is

$$\text{Call premium} = PV(F_0) \times N(d_1) - PV(E) \times N(d_2)$$
$$d_1 = \frac{\{\ln(F_0/E) + 0.5 \times (V^2) \times (T)\}}{[V \times \text{SQRT}(T)]}$$
$$d_2 = d_1 - V \times \text{SQRT}(T)$$

where $PV(\ )$ is present value using the riskless interest rate, F_0 is current futures price, $N(\ )$ is cumulative normal distribution function, E is exercise (strike) price, V is volatility, and T is time to expiration in years.

The formula requires only 5 inputs, three of which—current futures price, exercise price, and the option's time to expiration—are directly observable. A fourth input, the riskless interest rate, is not directly observable but can be estimated quite accurately by using comparable time duration U.S. government T-bills or T-notes. The fifth input, volatility, is more difficult to determine. Volatility is the annualized standard deviation of the rate of change of the cash market price over the period of the option's life. Because it is a prediction, it cannot be observed. It is possible, however, to estimate this input by using historical cash market data and assuming that this estimate will be acceptable for the period of the option's life.

Black and Scholes's formula can be used successfully to determine the price on nursery stock forward contract options. Many models, however, that will achieve the desired results are available. In addition, various easy-to-use software applications that can accomplish option pricing without requiring the user to have an advanced degree in mathematics are on the market.

10

Inventory, Hedging, and Speculating Strategies

The versatility of options stems from the variety of strategies available to the buyer (investor). Some of the more basic uses of options are explained in the following examples. For purposes of illustration, commission and transaction costs, tax considerations, and the costs involved in margin accounts, if applicable, have been omitted from the examples. These factors affect a strategy's potential outcome, so a buyer should always check with a broker and tax adviser before entering into any of these strategies.

The following examples also assume that all options are American style and, therefore, can be exercised at any time before expiration. In all the examples, the premiums used are reasonable but, in reality, will not necessarily exist at or prior to expiration for a similar option.

BUYING CALLS

Buying Calls as Part of an Inventory Plan

A popular use of options known as the "90/10 strategy" involves placing 10% of the inventory funds in long (purchased) calls and the other 90% in a secure investment such as a government bond or commercial paper (CP) until the option's expiration. This strategy provides both leverage (from the options) and limited risk (from the CP), allowing the investor to benefit from a favorable CP price move while limiting the downside risk to the call premium minus any interest earned from the CP.

Assume that black pine on the cash market is selling at $60 per tree. To purchase 100 trees would require an investment of $6,000, of which all would be exposed to basis risk. To employ the 90/10 strategy, a buyer would buy a 6-month 60 call. Assuming a premium of 6, the cost of the option would be $600. This leaves the investor with $5,400 to invest in CP with a 6-month maturity. Assuming that the estimated interest on the CP is 10%, the $5,400 would yield interest of $270 over the 6 months. The interest would effectively reduce the cost of the option to $330 ($600 premium minus $270 interest).

If the price of black pine increases on the cash market by 10% ($6) as demonstrated, the long call will realize the dollar appreciation at a long position's expiration in 100 trees but with less capital invested in the option than would have been invested in the 100 trees on the cash market. As a result, the buyer will realize a higher return on capital with the option than had he or she purchased 100 trees on the cash market and held them in inventory. Moreover, the cost to maintain the inventory over the 6-month period must be considered.

If the cash market price instead increases by less than $6 or if it falls, the loss will be limited to the price paid for the option. This loss, however, will be at least partially offset by the earned interest on the CP and, if the buyer chooses to do so, the premium received from selling the option. If the buyer elects to exercise the options, the CP funds are available to settle the forward contract.

Buying Calls to Lock in a Forward Contract Purchase Price

A buyer who sees an attractive cash market price but does not have sufficient cash flow to buy at the present time can use call options. Call options lock in a purchase price and guarantee supply on the forward market for future delivery or to hedge against future cash market prices.

Assume that black pine is currently selling for $50 per tree on the cash market and that a buyer wants to purchase 100 trees at this price for use in 6 months. This person, however, does not have the funds available now to secure the trees on the cash market. The necessary funds will be available in 6 months, but the buyer fears that the tree price will increase during this time.

Assume that the forward market price for delivery in 6 months is $55. One solution is to purchase a 6-month black pine call option at 55, thereby establishing the maximum price ($55 per tree). Assume that the option premium is $5.

If, as expected, the cash market price has risen to $70 in 6 months and sufficient funds are now available, the call option can be exercised. The buyer will then own 100 black pines at the option's strike price of $55. For a cost of $500 in option premium, he or she is able to buy trees at $5,500 rather than $7,000. The total cost is thus $6,000 ($5,500 + $500 premium), for a savings of $1,000 ($7,000 − $6,000).

Even though the buyer has paid $1,000 more on the forward market than on the cash market, assuming that the funds were available, the savings received from not having to pay the cost of capital, to maintain the trees for 6 months, to risk spoilage, and so forth become clear.

Now assume that instead of the cash market price raising to $70 as predicted, the price during the 6 months declined on the cash market to $45. Then the buyer would not want to exercise the call to buy at $55 because black pine can be bought on the cash market for $5 per tree less. The out-of-the-money call will either expire worthless or, to recoup a portion of its cost, can be sold for whatever time value it has remaining. The maximum loss with this strategy is the cost of the call option bought, $5.

Assume that the buyer purchased, with borrowed funds, black pine on the cash market for what was believed to be a good price, $50. The cost of 100 trees would have been $5,000.00. But the following would also have applied: interest for 6 months at 10% ($250) and 6 months' inventory carrying costs of at least $5 per tree ($500) gives a total acquisition cost of $5,750. Had the tree price on the cash market declined to $45, the loss would have been $1,250.

This assumes that there was no spoilage over the 6 months, which would increase the loss. So, attempting to save $1,000 raises the potential loss of at least $1,250. The point is that regardless of the price movement, up or down, the buyer successfully hedged and did so risking far less than had he or she purchased the material on the cash market.

Buying Calls to Hedge Short Cash Market Sales

A wholesaler, for example, who sold short on the cash market in anticipation of a price decline can limit a possible loss by purchasing call options. Remember that growers or wholesalers holding inventory for sale on the cash market will take orders on inventory from buyers at a set price, for delivery sometime in the near future. This is referred to as "shorting the cash market."

Assume that the wholesaler sold short (took orders on) 100 trees of black pine to a cash market buyer at $40 per tree. If the wholesaler buys a black pine 40 call at a premium of 4, he or she has established a maximum tree price of $40 that will have to be paid if the tree price rallies on the cash market, forcing the wholesaler to cover the short cash market position. For instance, if the cash market price at the time that delivery is to be made increases to $55 per tree, the value of the options held will increase accordingly. Thus the wholesaler can sell the option to realize gains lost from the short cash market sales.

Now assume that the option value has increased from 4 to 14. The original option purchase (4) and cash market sale (40) are offset as follows: $4,000 cash market sale + $1,400 (sell 100 call options at 14) − $400 original option purchase = $5,000. By hedging the cash market sale with call options, $1,000 was gained from the call option's increase in value.

The potential loss in this strategy is limited to the cost of the call, because if the call does not increase in value, the holder would not exercise the option.

SELLING CALLS

Upon being assigned an exercise notice, call writers are obligated to sell, at the strike price, the underlying trees. For example, assuming this obligation, a call writer is paid a premium at the time the call option is sold on the primary market. As discussed earlier, underwriters and broker members of the exchange introduce options on the primary market. All strike prices set for material supplied by the underwriter, as well as the option premium, are approved by the clearinghouse before introduction to the market. Strike prices are the prevailing prices for the contract month for delivery. Therefore, if an April contract is priced at $100, all those supplying material for that month receive $100.

Option Premium Distribution (Estimated)

46% NMR issuer (grower) and underwriter (negotiated prior to primary option introduction)

34% of premium to the SME

20% of premium to buyer's broker

Example: Assume a primary option premium of $420.

Underwriter and NMR issuer	$193.20
SME fees	$142.80
Buy broker's commission	$84.00
The client pays	$420.00 plus broker commissions.

Covered Call Writing

The most common strategy is writing calls against a long cash market position in the underlying tree, referred to as covered call writing.

Growers write covered calls primarily for the following reasons:

1. They have new markets to which to sell material.

2. They receive 10% to 15% more than cash market sales, with no associated sales or marketing costs.

3. They can realize additional return on excess inventory not committed to cash market sales (premium income).

4. They can gain some protection (limited to the amount of the premium) from a decline in tree price.

5. If assigned an exercise notice, payment is immediate.

6. If cash market increase options can be purchased to cancel delivery obligations, material can be sold on the cash market.

Covered call writing is a more conservative strategy because the writer's downside risk is slightly offset by the premium received for selling the call on trees they own. Covered call writers own the trees but may be willing to forsake cash market price increases in excess of the option strike price in return for the premium. They must be prepared, however, to deliver the necessary trees to fulfill the underlying forward contract (if assigned) at any time during the life of the option. Of course, by executing a closing transaction (that is, by buying a call in the same series), they may cancel their obligations at any time before being assigned an exercise notice. This transaction eliminates the obligation to satisfy delivery on a forward contract.

A covered call writer's potential profits and losses are influenced by the strike price of the call he or she chooses to sell. In all cases, the writer's maximum net gain will be realized if the tree price on the cash market is at or above the strike price of the option at expiration or at assignment.

Assuming that the tree's strike price is equal to the tree's current price:

1. If a covered call writer writes an at-the-money call (strike price equal to the current price of the long position), the maximum net gain is the premium received for selling the option.
2. If an in-the-money call (strike price less than the current price of the long position is written, the maximum net gain is the premium minus the difference between the tree purchase price and the strike price.
3. If an out-of-the-money call (strike price greater than the current cash market price of the tree is written, the maximum net gain is the premium plus the difference between the strike price and the tree purchase price should the cash market price increase above the strike price.

If the writer is assigned an exercise notice, the profit or loss is determined by the amount of the premium received plus the difference, if any, between the strike price and the original tree price on the cash market. If the tree price on the cash market rises above the strike price of the option and the writer has the contract called away (that is, the contract is assigned), the opportunity to profit from further increases in the tree price is sacrificed.

Assume that a black pine April 50 call is written at a premium of 5 covered by 100 trees purchased on the cash market, or value for material held in inventory, at $50 per tree. The premium received helps to fulfill one objective as of a call writer: additional income from inventory. In this example, a $5 per tree premium represents a 10% yield on the $50 per tree value. Now, depending on the agreement with the underwriter, the investor can receive, for example, 50% of the option premium of $250.

If the tree price on the cash market subsequently declines to $40, the long tree position will decrease in value by $1,000. This unrealized loss will be partially offset by the $250 in premium received for writing the call. In other words, if the tree on the cash market is actually sold at $40, the opportunity loss will be only $750.

On the other hand, if the tree price on the cash market rises to $60 and an exercise notice is assigned, the writer must sell the 100 trees for $5,000. By writing a call option, the opportunity to profit from an increase in value of the long position in excess of the strike price of the option is lost. The $250 in premium is kept, however, results in a net selling price of $5,250. The $7.50 per tree difference between this net selling price ($52.50) and the current market value ($60) of the tree represents the "opportunity cost" of writing this call option.

Of course, a writer is not limited to writing an option with a strike price equal to the price at which the tree was bought or valued. Instead, he or she might choose a strike price below the current market price of the inventory (that is, an in-the-money option). Because the option buyer is already getting part of the desired benefit—appreciation above the strike price—he or she will be willing to pay a higher premium, which will provide a greater measure of downside protection. The writer, however, will also have assumed a greater chance that the call will be exercised.

On the other hand, the writer could opt for writing a call option with a strike price that is above the current market price of the inventory (that is, an out-of-the-money option). Because this lowers the option buyer's chances of benefiting from the investment, the premium will be lower, as will the chances that the inventory will be called away.

In short, the writer of a covered call option, in return for the premium received, forgoes the opportunity to benefit from an increased tree price that exceeds the strike price of the option, but continues to bear the risk of a sharp decline in the value of the inventory, which will only be slightly offset by the premium received for selling the option.

UNCOVERED CALL WRITING

SME does not currently allow uncovered call trading, and it may be years before the clearinghouse allows uncovered or naked option writing. The reasons are many; one is market integrity. For educational purposes, however, this text now discusses uncovered call options.

A call option writer is uncovered if he or she does not own the nursery stock of the underlying forward contract represented by the option. An uncovered call writer's objective is to realize income from the writing transaction without committing capital to the ownership of the underlying nursery stock. An uncovered option is also referred to as a naked option. Typically, an uncovered call writer must deposit and maintain sufficient cash to ensure that the inventory can be purchased for delivery if and when an exercise notice is assigned.

Writing uncovered calls can be profitable or generally stable during periods of declining prices, but writers considering this strategy should recognize the significant risks involved. For instance, if the cash market price of the inventory rises sharply, the calls could be exercised. To satisfy the delivery obligation, the writer may have to acquire inventory in the cash market for more than the option's strike price. This could result in a substantial loss.

The risk of writing uncovered calls is similar to that of selling inventory short, although the option writer's risk is cushioned somewhat by the amount of premium received. For example, if a black pine April 65 call is written for a premium of 6, $300 in premium income (6 × 100 trees − 50% underwriter fees) will be received. If on the cash market the inventory price remains at or below $65, an exercise notice will not be assigned on the option and, because the writer has no inventory position, the price decline has no effect on the $300 profit. On the other hand, if the price subsequently climbs to $75 per tree, an exercise option will likely be assigned and the writer will have to cover his or her position at a loss of $700 ($1,000 loss on covering the call assignment offset by $300 in premium income). To cover delivery of the forward contract, the writer had to buy trees on the cash market for $75 per tree.

As with any option transaction, by executing a closing purchase transaction (purchase options in the same series), an uncovered call writer may cancel his or her obligation at any time before being assigned an exercise notice. An uncovered call writer can also mitigate the risk at any time during the life of the option by purchasing the underlying trees, thereby becoming a covered writer.

BUYING PUT OPTIONS

A put option contract gives its holder the right to sell a forward contract at the given strike price on or before the expiration date of the contract.

Buying Puts to Participate in Downward Price Movements

Put options may provide a more attractive method of profiting on declines in tree price than selling inventory on the cash market in that purchased puts have a known and predetermined risk. The most money that can be lost, if the price goes up on the cash market, is the cost of the option; the put seller would not exercise the put if the price increases. If, however, the cash market price declines below the put's strike price, the seller is obligated to buy. With selling inventory on the cash market, the potential opportunity loss, in the event of a price increase, is unlimited.

Assume a grower sells (takes orders on) inventory on the cash market months before delivery because he or she believes that the price may be lower at the time the tree is ready for delivery. During the period between the order is taken at, for instance, 40 and the time the inventory is ready for delivery, however, the price on the cash market increases 10 above the price originally agreed upon for selling the inventory on the cash market. The anticipated gain by selling early has, in fact, developed into an opportunity loss of $10. A put buyer (a grower), however, can hold his or her position through the option's expiration without incurring any additional risk.

Buying an April 40 put gives the put buyer the right to sell 100 black pines at $40 per tree at any time before the option expires in April. This right to sell trees at a fixed price becomes more valuable as the price for black pine/ declines.

Assume that the price of the underlying trees as $40 at the time the option was bought and that the premium paid was 4 (or $400). If the price of black pine on the cash market falls to $35 before April and if the premium rises to 6, there are two choices for disposing the in-the-money put option:

1. Buy 100 trees on the cash market at $35 per tree and simultaneously exercise the put option to sell black pine at $40 per tree, netting a profit of $100 ($500 profit on the trees less the $400 option premium).
2. Sell the put option contract, collecting the difference between the premium paid and the premium received, which in this case is $200.

The profitability of similar examples depends on how the time remaining until expiration affects the premium. Remember that time value declines sharply as an option nears its expiration date.

If black pine prices on the cash market had instead climbed to $45 prior to expiration and if the premium had fallen to $3, the put option would be out of the money. The option could still be sold for $300, partially offsetting its original price. In most cases, the cost of this strategy will be less than what would have been lost had the buyer shorted black pine on the cash market instead of purchasing the put option (in this case, $100 versus $500).

This strategy allows a grower to benefit from downward price movements while limiting losses to the premium paid if prices increase.

Buying Puts to Protect a Long Position

The risk of inventory ownership can be limited by simultaneously buying a put on that inventory, a hedging strategy commonly referred to as a "married put." This strategy establishes a minimum selling price for the trees during the life of the put and limits the buyer's loss to the cost of the put plus the difference, if any, between the purchase price of the trees and the strike price of the put, no matter how far the tree price declines. A married put will yield a profit if the tree appreciation is greater than the cost of the put option.

Assume that 100 trees of black pine are bought at $40 per tree and, at some time, an April 40 put at a premium of 4 is also bought. For the $400 in premium, the buyer has ensured that no matter what happens to the price of the trees, he or she will be able to sell 100 trees for $40 per tree, or $4,000 total.

If the price of black pine increases to $50 per tree and the premium of the option drops to 3, the inventory position is now worth $5,000 but the put is out of the money. The profit, if the inventory is sold, is $600 ($1,000 profit on the trees less the $400 paid for the put option). If the price increase occurs before expiration, however, the loss on the put can be reduced by selling it for whatever time value remains, in this case, $300 if the July 40 put can be sold.

If the price of black pine instead falls to $30 per tree, the inventory position would only be worth $3,000 (an unrealized loss of $1,000). The buyer, however, could exercise the put, selling the inventory for $40 per tree to break even on the inventory position, at a cost of $400 (the premium paid for the put).

This strategy is a significant method for hedging a long inventory position. Although the buyer is fully protected against downside risk, there is no ceiling on the upside profit potential.

Buying Puts to Protect Unrealized Profit in Long Inventory

If a buyer has an established profitable long inventory position, he or she can buy puts to protect this position against short-term price declines. If the price of the inventory declines by more than the cost of the put, the put can be sold or exercised to offset this decline. If the buyer decides to exercise the put, the inventory can be sold at the put option's strike price, no matter how far the inventory price has declined.

Assume that black pine was bought on the cash market at $60 per tree and that the current price is $75 per tree. By buying a black pine put option with a strike price of $70 for a premium of 2, a buyer is assured of being able to sell the inventory at $70 per tree during the life of the option. The profit, of course, would be reduced by the $200 paid for the put.

For example, if the tree price on the cash market drops to $65 and if the premium increases to 6, the put could be exercised and the inventory sold for $70 per tree. The $1,000 profit on the inventory position would be offset by the cost of the put option, resulting in a profit of $800.

Alternatively, if the buyer wishes to maintain his or her position in the inventory, the in-the-money put could be sold for $600 and the difference between the premiums received and paid, $400 in this case, could be collected, which might offset some of or all the lost inventory value.

If the inventory price were to climb, there would be no limit to the potential profit from the tree's increase in price. This gain on the inventory, however, would be reduced by the cost of the put.

SELLING PUT OPTIONS

Selling a put obligates the individual to buy the underlying trees at the option's strike price upon assignment of an exercise notice. To compensate the seller for assuming this risk, a premium is paid when the put is written. A put writer must be prepared to buy the underlying trees at any time during the life of the option. Simply stated, the put buyer is hedging against lower price, and the put seller is banking on higher prices in hopes that the put goes unexercised.

COVERED PUT WRITING

A put writer is considered to be covered if he or she has a corresponding short position. For purposes of cash account transactions, a put writer is also considered to be covered if he or she deposits cash or cash equivalents or holds inventory equal to the exercise value of the option. A covered put writer's profit potential is limited to the premium received plus the difference between the strike price of the put and the original cost of the short position.

The potential loss on this position, however, is substantial if the price of the cash market increases significantly above the original price of the short position. In this case, the short position will accrue losses but the offsetting profit on the put sale is limited to the premium received.

UNCOVERED PUT WRITING

A put writer is considered to be uncovered if he or she does not have a corresponding short position, has not deposited cash, or does not hold inventory equal to the exercise value of the put. Like uncovered call writing, uncovered put writing has limited rewards (the premium received) and potentially substantial risk (if prices fall and the put is assigned). The primary motivations for most put writers are to receive premium income and to acquire inventory at a net cost below the current market value.

If the cash market price declines below the strike price of the put and if the put is exercised, the put writer will be obligated to buy the inventory at the strike price. The cost will, of course, be offset at least partially by the premium received for writing the option. If the cash market price rises instead, the put will most likely expire.

Assume that a black pine April 55 put is written for a premium of 5 and that the market price of black pine on the cash market subsequently drops from $55 to $45 per tree. If the put is assigned, the buyer must buy 100 trees at a cost of $5,500; the net effect, however, is $5000 because of the $500 premium income received. Had the market price of black pine remained at or above $55, it is highly unlikely that the put would be assigned, and the $500 premium would be the profit.

Conclusion

This book's intended purpose was to provide an introduction to SME and the fundamentals of buying, selling, and holding options and to illustrate some of the basic strategies available to the nursery industry. Exchange-traded options have many benefits, including flexibility, leverage, limited risk for buyers, and guaranteed contract performance. Options allow the nursery professional to participate in price movements without committing the large amount of funds needed to buy inventory outright on the cash market. Options can also be used to hedge a cash market position, to acquire or sell inventory at a purchase price more favorable than the current cash market price, or in the case of writing options, to earn premium income.

Whether buying for inventory, hedging price or supply, or even speculating, a broker can help select an appropriate options strategy. The strategies presented here do not cover all, or even a significant number of, the strategies possible to use options. These most basic strategies, however, will serve as building blocks for the more complex strategies available.

Despite their many benefits, options are not suitable for everyone. A buyer who wants to use options should have well-defined goals suited to his or her particular financial situation as well as a plan for achieving these objectives. The successful use of options requires a willingness to learn what they are, how they work, and what risks are associated with particular options strategies.

With an understanding of the fundamentals, individuals seeking new opportunities to improve their nursery operations will find options trading challenging and potentially rewarding.

Seattle Mercantile Exchange Quick Reference Guide for Risk Management

The following is a quick reference guide of the nursery industry's needs and risk management strategies offered by Seattle Mercantile Exchange (SME) contracts:

Landscape Brokers: Usually represent various nurseries and sell the nurseries' material directly to the customer. Customers are anyone in the nursery trade.
Needs: B, C, D, F.

Wholesalers (Rewholesalers): "Buy-in" nursery stock from growers, store on site, and sell to the trade.
Needs: A, B, C, D, E, F, G.

Landscape Contractors: Purchase and install nursery stock.
Needs: B, D, G.

Landscape Architects: Educated in design, construction techniques, and horticultural practices.
Needs: C, D.

Developers: Those that build large residential, commercial, or industrial developments.
Needs: C, D.

Garden Centers/Retailers: "Buy-in" nursery stock, sell to the public.
Needs: B, C, D, G.

Growers/Nurserymen: Own and/or operate a nursery or a growing operation.
Needs: A, B, C, D, E, F, G.

There are many reasons for each segment of the industry to trade on the SME; these outlined are but a few. As trading evolves, new ideas and benefits will surface.

[A] Need: A market to sell inventory at market prices. Inherently, there is an excess of material at the close of a selling season.

Two main reasons:

- Canceled orders—about 5%
- Excess inventory—about 5%

Solution: Determine the amount of excess material for each season, then place onto the forward market.

Benefits:

- No cost associated with placing material.
- Receive compensation from primary option sales.
- If an option expires, a grower can return material back onto the forward market or sell the material on the cash market.
- Compensation for a forward contract = the full strike price. (No need to lower prices to sell inventory.)

Reservations: Placing material onto the forward market would tie up inventory that could potentially have a cash market buyer.

Answers to that concern:

- The grower can always buy back the option(s) covering the material placed onto the forward market. For instance, if the grower has a cash market buyer willing to pay more than the forward contracts strike price, the grower could buy options covering the placed material; thereby the obligation to make delivery on the forward contract is released and the material can be sold to the cash market customer.
- Only place estimated excess inventory onto the forward market (i.e., inventory that normally would be discarded or used as a "special" item).

Note: A "grower" can be anyone that can guarantee the delivery of material for a forward contract. For example, if a landscape broker can secure inventory from a nursery, he or she can place material onto the forward market. A retailer with excess inventory could also place material onto the forward market. This holds true for other segments of the industry that hold excess inventory.

[B] Need: A way to control inventory. Currently, buyers "order in" enough stock to cover projected needs. Since this is just a projection, and given that the harvesting of most plant material is seasonal, there is a chance that material will run out, or worse yet, the buyer could get caught with too much material. The buyer needs flexibility to acquire additional material or "fill-ins" to supplement current inventories without added expense and/or risk of over- or understocking.

Solution: Buy on the cash market for early needs (e.g., January, April, August, October), supplement with options for the next contract date, and exercise to forwards as needed. This works especially well for fall needs. By buying option contracts for the following spring, then exercising early, the buyer will receive the same sized material as they would have in the spring.

This strategy helps the buyer in the following ways:

- It provides a way to obtain fresh stock.
- It cuts down on inventory carrying costs.

Additional benefits: As buyers print catalogs and/or availability lists based on salable inventory, buying options offer opportunities to do the following:

- Presell by including material in sales catalogs.
- Try new material.

- Cover shortages.
- Let current material grow on.

Reservations: What happens if the additional material does not sell? Exercise options only for material needed and trade the balance of the option contracts. If more material is needed, buy forward contracts or buy on the cash market.

[C] Need: Guaranteed prices. Given that pricing throughout the nursery industry is volatile, options allow the buyer to secure pricing for both current and future needs.

Solution: Buy options as a price hedge against the cash market. Some practical applications are as follows:

- Growers or rewholesalers who only print a yearly catalog would have an advantage against an increase in cash market prices for the next season.
- Landscape brokers and garden centers would have a way to lock in prices so that they can set up yearly promotion schedules.
- Landscape contractors, landscape architects, and developers can set fixed budgets for future projects.

Reservations: What happens if the material is not needed or can be purchased on the cash market for less than the forward market?

- Sell the options and buy on the cash market.
- Let the option expire.
- Remember options are an insurance policy against price increases and supply uncertainty.

[D] Need: A guaranteed method for receiving quality nursery stock in the exact quantity ordered and to do so more efficiently, rather than spending hours or days shopping for and securing the best values.

Solution: Use the forward market to purchase more efficiently. Buying options and forward contracts offer a buyer more flexibility. Other opportunities with options:

- Try new products, without the fear of receiving inferior product.
- Increase quantities. Try out new marketing strategies without the fear of over-inventorying.
- Supplement existing material. For instance, a grower could let current field material "size up" or "grow on" by supplementing with options.

Note: SME is committed to supplying consistent quality nursery stock year in and year out. With the industry's best growers placing material onto the forward market and with the exchange's quality controls, a buyer is guaranteed quality at competitive pricing, in the exact quantities ordered.

- Strict guidelines are used in accepting material onto the forward market.
- All underwriters are accountable and financially responsible for the material they place onto the forward market.
- Horticultural experts verify the quality and quantity of the product to be shipped.
- Growers are financially obligated to ship only quality material.
- The exchange is dedicated to selecting only the best growers.

[E] Need: A way to expand market penetration and increase sales more efficiently without increasing overhead costs. There is only so much ground one can cover. Small or even large companies cannot get to everyone.

Solution: Utilize the SME's national (international) sales representation. SME can reach more buyers, without the expense of expanding or creating a sales force.

- There is no cost to place material on the exchange.
- There are no additional commissions or discounts to pay.

Reservations: The exchange might take business away from the current cash market sales.

- On the contrary, SME would serve as a way to obtain greater quantities of material at no risk and no expense. By placing material onto the forward market, a grower can receive greater revenues then currently received from cash market sales. At the same time, growers can create a better working relationship with others to whom they are currently selling, such as wholesalers and landscape brokers.
- In addition, there is other genus not traded by SME.
- There is a market for material not exercised by an option holder.

[F] Need: A better way to manage cash flow. Growers need a way to be paid sooner, for all material shipped.

Solution: SME provides a more efficient way for growers to be paid then offered by the cash market. The exchange helps with cash flow problems. It does the following:

- Pays the day the truck is loaded
- Pays the exact strike price

- Guarantees the material to the customer; there is no need for credits
- Pays on the sale of primary options, thereby providing the grower with working capital

[G] **Need:** A way to increase prices to profitable levels.

Solution: As the amount of material traded increases, buyers will look to the forward market for purchasing needs. SME offers the market equal access for price discovery. Middleman mark-ups are not inherent on the forward market, therefore, growers and end-users benefit from direct forward market purchases.

Glossary

The terms, phrases, and words used to trade or to describe transactions conducted on an exchange often seem foreign to most observers. Puts, calls, covered, and naked are but a few of those bewildering, but innocuous words. Over the years, the "communication art" of trading has taken on its own identity. As in many industries, however, a language often develops and becomes the accepted norm of the industry.

For those new to trading on a commodity exchange, exchange communication can be confusing and frustrating He's "long" the market or she's "short" the market may not mean anything. When conducting business with a member broker, use the language of the industry as often as possible. If a term used by a broker is unclear, however, ask the broker to explain exactly what is meant. Brokers are there to assist buyers and sellers. When in doubt about the meaning of a particular word or phrase, always remember to ask for a clarification.

Abandon: To let an option expire unexercised. This usually occurs if an option is worthless. That is, the option's strike price is higher than the cash market.

American-style option: An option contract that can be exercised at any time between the date of purchase and the expiration date.

Ask: The amount a seller would like to receive for his or her option or forward contract.

Assignment: The receipt of an exercise notice by an option writer that obligates him or her to sell (in the case of a call) or purchase (in the case of a put) the underlying security at the specified strike price.

Associate member(ship): Sponsored by a charter member, an Associate Member, typically a large-volume transaction client (e.g., a landscape broker or wholesaler), has direct trading privileges with the exchange for his or her own account but can not open new accounts. Trading is limited to selected commodities and membership fees are based on the commodity(s) selected and trading volumes.

At-the-money: An option whose strike price is equal—or approximately equal—to the current cash market price of the underlying forward contract.

Basis: The difference between a local cash market price and a forward market price of a particular forward contract.

Basis risk: The risk that basis may be greater than or less than the amount planned for.

Bearish: A market view that anticipates lower prices.

Bid: The price a buyer is willing to pay for an option or forward contract.

Break-even point: The forward price at which a given option strategy is neither profitable or unprofitable. For call options, it is the strike price plus the premium and related trading commissions. For put options, it is the strike price minus the premium and related trading commissions.

Broker: Individual who executes or trades options and/or forward contracts for clients on the Seattle Mercantile Exchange. (See **Charter Member** and **Associate Member.**)

Bullish: A market view that anticipates higher prices.

Buyer: The purchaser of an option or forward contract. The buyer may also be referred to as the *holder.*

Call option: An option that gives the option buyer the right (not obligation) to purchase (go "long") an underlying forward contract at the strike price on or before the expiration date.

Carrying charge: Cost of maintaining inventory, including fertilizers, water, labor, taxes, and finance costs. Could also include the costs for storing material in containers for closed harvest deliveries.

Cash account: Unlike a margin account, cash has to be on deposit for trading or cash has to be available when a trade is made and settled.

Cash market: A type of market where a physical transfer of a product takes place the same time payment is made. A cash market is also known as a *spot market.*

Charter member(ship): Being a charter member, or founding member of Seattle Mercantile Exchange, entitles the holder to all rights and privileges of the exchange. Membership allows for trading in all commodities and for setting up new clients and sponsoring associate members.

Class of options: Option contracts of the same type (call or put) and style (American or European) that cover the same underlying forward contract.

Clearinghouse: The essential purpose of the clearinghouse is to guarantee the performance on all contracts traded. The clearinghouse takes no active position in the market, but interposes itself between all parties to every transmission. It serves this role when a buy-and-sell trade relationship is established on the exchange. The clearinghouse function is under the direct supervision of the SME.

Closed harvest period: Times when there are natural (i.e., biological) constraints on the harvesting of material. (See **Open harvest period.**)

Closing purchase: A transaction in which the purchaser's intention is to reduce or eliminate the short position in a given series of options.

Closing sale: A transaction in which the seller's intention is to reduce or eliminate the long position in a given series of options.

Commercial hedger: A trader who is directly involved with the industry for which contracts are offered. Commercial hedgers trade to offset risk in their cash market positions.

Commissions: Fees charged to clients by member brokerage firms for trades conducted on behalf of the client. Commission rates are set by the member brokerage firm.

Commission broker: A broker who works for a member broker.

Commodity: Anything that can be bought or sold. The term commodity is typically associated with items traded on an exchange.

Computer trading: Unlike the open-out cry on many exchanges, SME trades are executed on the National Computerized Trading System (NCTS) developed by the SME.

Contract: An agreement between at least two parties. A contract usually involves a buyer and a seller and includes certain specifications. Different types of contracts are available in the cash and forward markets.

Contract month: The month an option contract expires, or in the case of a forward contract, the month in which the contract's underlying nursery stock will be delivered. Option contract months are April and October; forward contract delivery months are May and November.

Contract specifications: A document that describes in detail, for example, the nursery material being offered for trade on an exchange, the contract's expiration and trading dates, grading methods, other pertinent information regarding trading procedures, and the related nursery material being traded. Contract specifications are written for options and forward contracts.

Covered call option writing: A short call option position in which the writer owns the nursery stock of the underlying forward contract represented by the option contracts.

Covered put option writing: A short put option position in which the writer is also short the corresponding nursery stock or has deposited, in a cash account, cash or cash equivalents equal to the exercise value of the option.

Covered writing: A call or put on a forward contract in which the writer has an opposite cash market position; that is, the writer owns or has guaranteed access to the underlying commodity. (See **Pool.**)

Current cash price: see **Local cash price.**

Delivery: The physical transfer of a commodity. Delivery is made under specific terms and procedures established by the clearinghouse upon which the commodity is traded. Make or take delivery are terms used to describe the delivery transaction.

Delta (Δ): The amount by which an option premium will change for a corresponding change in the underlying commodity's forward price.

Demand: The amount of nursery material buyers want to purchase on either the cash or forward market.

Derivative: A financial instrument (such as an option) whose value is derived in part from the value and characteristics of the underlying forward contract.

European-style option: An option contract that can only be exercised on the expiration date.

Even basis: A market condition that exists when the local cash price is equal to the forward price. Also referred to as *no basis.*

Exchange: A centralized market where trading of options, forward or futures contracts for securities, and agricultural and precious metal commodities are conducted.

Exercise: The action taken by the holder of a call if he or she wishes to purchase the underlying forward contract, or by the holder of a put if he or she wishes to sell the underlying forward contract.

Exercise price: see **Strike price.**

Expiration date: The last date on which an option may be exercised on the last day for delivery on a forward contract. On this date all rights of the option holder and all obligations of the issuer cease.

Extrinsic value: see **Time value.**

Forward contract: A contract that is predicated on the holder or writer "taking and making" delivery on the underlying commodity, for a specific price, delivery date, and quantity. In 99% of trades conducted on the Seattle Mercantile Exchange, the underlying commodity of the forward contracts is delivered. Payment in full by the buyer (settlement) is made prior to the granting of a forward contract.

Future (forward) price: The price of a particular commodity at some future time and date.

Futures contract: A contract traded on a futures exchange for the delivery of a specified commodity at a future time. The contract specifies the material to be delivered, the price, and the terms and conditions of delivery. In 99% of transactions, the underlying commodity of a futures contract is not delivered. A futures contract is typically traded, or opposite positions in the market are taken to offset the futures contract's commodity delivery requirements.

Futures (forward) market: The place where financial instruments for the future delivery of commodities are bought and sold.

Grading method: A method that outlines, for example, the caliper, height, spread, and other pertinent specifications regarding the particulars of the plant species traded on the SME. The specifications criteria and grading method are set by the exchange according to the American Standard for Nursery Stock (ASNS) offered by the American Association of Nurseryman (AAN).

Grantor: see **Seller.**

Grower: An individual or firm who grows nursery/landscape material. (See **Member grower.**)

Hedge: The buying or selling of offsetting positions to provide protection against an adverse change in price to guarantee supply or a sale. A hedge may involve having positions in the cash, forward, or options markets.

In-the-money: A call option, for example, is in the money if the option's price is below the current cash market price of the option's underlying forward contract (that is, if the option has intrinsic value). A put option is in the money if the option's strike price is above the current cash market price of the put option's underlying forward contract.

Intrinsic value: The dollar amount that would be realized if the option were to be exercised immediately. (See **In the money.**)

Introducing broker: A broker who is not a member of an exchange, but who uses a member broker to clear trades. Introducing brokers develop and trade for their own clients.

Lapsed option: A put or call option that has expired unexercised.

Letter of credit: A written document issued by banks or other similar financial institutions. Letters of credit guarantee payment of an individual's or company's obligation.

Lifting a hedge: The buying (selling) back of material rights from (to) the forward market. Lifting a hedge is the removal of offsetting positions designed to protect against adverse price-level changes.

Limit order: An order that sets the highest price the customer is willing to be paid or the lowest price acceptable for sale. Buy orders may be executed at or below the limit price, but never higher. Sell orders may be executed at or above the limit price, but never lower.

Local cash price: The price at which nursery material can be bought at or sold on the cash market. (See **Cash market.**)

Long: The position that is established by the purchase or ownership of a forward contract, commodity, or option if there is no offsetting position.

Markdown: The charge subtracted by a firm, acting as principal, from the price on a sell transaction.

Market: The interactions of individuals and firms buying and selling.

Market order: Instructions from a customer to his or her broker to buy or sell at the market's price.

Market maker: A broker member who buys options at a bid price or sells at an offer price. Market markers offer liquidity by stepping into the market to meet otherwise unfilled orders. Market makers support option pricing equilibrium and are obligated to enter the market to keep prices from falling or raising sharply.

Mark-up: The charge imposed by a firm, acting as a principal, on a buy transaction.

Material: Actual landscape/nursery commodities such as trees and bushes.

Member grower: A grower of nursery/landscape material who is contractually bound to the clearinghouse to supply material to the pool. (See **pool.**)

Naked writing: Writing a call or put option on a forward contract in which the writer has no opposite cash market position; an offsetting position. This is also known as *uncovered writing.* The writer does not own or have guaranteed access to the underlying commodity.

Nearby basis: The difference between the current cash price and the price of the forward contract with the nearest expiration date.

Negative basis: see **Under basis.**

Nursery material receipt (NMR): An agreement issued by the SME Clearing House to a member grower when the grower desires to place material into the pool (see **pool**). An NMR outlines the quantity, grade, and other information pertaining to the nursery material being supplied to the pool. An NMR indicates the date by which the grower would like the material sold and the strike price the grower will receive when the grower "makes delivery" of the material described by the NMR. An NMR can cover as few as 25 plants to as many as the clearinghouse is accepting for placement on the forward market. An NMR is issued only by the Seattle Mercantile Exchange Clearing House.

Offsetting position: Having a position in the opposite side of a transaction, such as being long the commodity.

Open harvest period: Times when there are no natural (i.e., biological) constraints on the harvesting of material.

Opening purchase: A transaction in which the purchaser's intention is to create or increase a long position in a given series of options.

Open interest: The number of outstanding option contracts in the forward market or in a particular class or series.

Open sale: A transaction in which the seller's intention is to create or increase a short position in a given series of options.

Option: The right, but not the obligation, to buy (in the case of a call option) or sell (in the case of a put option) an underlying forward contract under specific conditions. For this right the option holder pays to the option seller a price (premium). (See **Call option** and **Put option.**)

Out of the money: A put or call option that currently has no intrinsic value. That is, a call whose strike price is above the current forward price or a put whose strike price is below the current forward price.

Over basis: A market condition that exists when the local cash price is above the forward price. Also referred to as *positive basis.*

Pool: Nursery material committed to the Seattle Mercantile Exchange Clearing House to cover options and forward contracts traded on the exchange. Nursery material is supplied by various growers throughout the United States and Canada.

Position: Market position; the term used to describe an individual's exchange involvement. If an individual is attempting to buy or sell contracts on an exchange, he or she has a position.

Positive basis: see **Over basis.**

Premium: The price of a particular option contract that is determined initially by underwriters and later by competition between buyers and sellers on the secondary market. The premium is the maximum amount of potential loss to which the option buyer may be subject.

Price-level risk: The risk that, at time of actual sale (or purchase) of material, the price received (or paid) may be higher or lower than expected.

Primary market: The original underwriting, introduction, and trading of options or forward contract on an exchange.

Put option: An option that gives the option buyer the right to sell (go "short") the underlying forward contract at the strike price on or before the option's expiration date.

Secondary market: Trading (reselling and buying) on an exchange of the original options or forward contracts prior to the option's or contract's assigned expiration date.

Seller: Also known as *option writer* or *grantor.* The seller of an option is subject to a potential obligation, such as supplying the commodity, if the option holder chooses to exercise the option.

Series: All option contracts of the same class that also have the same unit of trade, expiration date, and exercise price.

Settlement: The term used to describe the closing of a transaction when payments are made, financial instruments are conveyed, and so forth.

Settlement date: The day when a transaction is to be completed (settled). On this day, the buyer is to pay and the seller is to deliver the commodity.

Short: The position created by the sale of a forward contract or option.

Specialty department: An exchange department that writes and introduces options on the primary market; used primarily for trading efficiency.

Spot market: see **Cash market.**

Spread: The difference between two forward prices.

Stop limit order: Similar to a stop order but one that becomes a limit order instead of a market order. "Buy" stop limit orders are entered above the current market; "sell" stops are extended below it.

Stop order: A special type of order that becomes a market order when the price is reached or passed. "Buy stops" are entered above the current market price; "sell stops" are entered below it.

Storage: The holding of material for sale at a later date.

Strengthening: A type of basis movement when the cash price is increasing relative to the forward price over time. Short hedgers benefit from this type of basis movement. Also known as a *narrowing of the basis.*

Strike price: The price at which the holder of a call or put option may choose to exercise the right to buy (sell) the underlying forward contract. Also known as the *exercise price.*

Supply: Material available for sale on either the cash of forward market.

Time value: The amount by which an option's premium exceeds the option's intrinsic value. If an option has no intrinsic value, its premium is entirely time value.

Track country station price: The price paid for a commodity loaded for delivery at a grower's site.

Transfer agent: A person who handles account transactions as well as the transfer and escrow of funds.

Type: The classification of an option contract as either a put or a call.

Uncovered writing: see **Naked Writing.**

Under basis: A market condition that exists when the local cash price is less than the forward price. Also referred to as *negative basis.*

Underlying: The forward contract behind an option or the commodity underlying a forward contract.

Underwriter: A person who writes and introduces options on an Exchange for the primary market. Underwriters provide a competitive pricing mechanism for the sale of hedging opportunities. Underwriters assess the benefits of the risk transference associated with their options and use this assessment to establish premium levels. They are paid a fee for introducing options on the primary market.

Volatility: Market movement or market risk.

Weakening: A type of basis movement when the cash price is declining relative to the forward price over time. Long hedgers benefit from this type of basis movement. Also known as *widening of the basis.*

Widening of the basis: see **Weakening.**

Writer: see **Seller.**

Appendix

TRADING RESOURCES

PMI
7169 South Braden Avenue
Tulsa, Oklahoma 74136
918-492-3007

The *Options Trader* is a user-driven, structured decision-making and education software package. Options Trader guides the user through a tutorial process that teaches the nursery professional how best to incorporate options trading into existing business plans. It presents the problems the nursery industry encounters with cash market transactions and develops the most effective option strategies for shifting risk. For product information, contact PMI directly.

Commodity Trading Institute (CTI)
27 Cleveland Avenue
Valhalia, New York 10595
1-800-770-0234

CTI is an education provider serving the needs of the nursery industry. In addition to producing trading seminars for the nursery industry, CTI publishes the *CTI Journal* (the official publication of the Seattle Mercantile Exchange). The *CTI Journal* is the only magazine that gives nursery professionals the information needed to trade SME options and forward contracts.

Each issue previews educational books, analytical software, and seminars that can guide individuals on the nuances of how to trade SME contracts. In addition, *CTI Journal* offers readers insightful articles on SME market trends, national and regional business issues, as well as market overviews to help nursery professionals improve profit performance. Advertisers are companies that offer educational products as well as services for traders.

Other CTI Services

Market Quotes by Phone: Receive, for any one genus traded
on SME, day-week hi-low quotes, last trades, and option and contract month strike prices.

Market Quotes by Fax: Receive, for all genus traded, a complete update of the week's activity, including day-week
hi-low quotes, last trades, and option and contract
month strike prices.

For product information contact CTI directly.

Founder's Letter
One Padanaram Road 207
Danbury, Connecticut 06811
1-800-888-2028, ext 150

The Founder's Letter, produced weekly and faxed to clients, is an in-depth analytical newsletter that offers trading
strategies and buy-and-sell recommendations. Published
by David R. Capasso and staff, with a panel of SME member contributors, the letter is written for active traders and
those needing additional market advice.

The Founder's Letter researches and analyzes national and regional consumer demand and grower supply trends to furnish subscribers with financial and
market-related facts to assist with making buy or sell
market decisions. In addition, the Founder's Letter offers
insight into future cash, forward market, and option
pricing.

Studies demonstrate that 40% of nursery stock sold in
the United States is influenced by landscape architects.
An additional 30% is influenced by landscape contractors.
Who better to talk to about consumer demands than those
industry segments that influence 70% of the nursery material sold annually. The Founder's Letter is in contact with
landscape architects and contractors from across the

United States to determine how design considerations will have an impact on genus demand, grower supply, and the related pricing of those genus studied, and reports these facts to subscribers.

SME MEMBERS

WESTERN REGION

First Pacific Commodities
5226 108th St. SW
Mukliteo, WA 98275
206-270-7588

Leonhardt and Associates
2422 E. Aloha Street
Seattle, WA 98112
206-233-8157

San Francisco Trading Co.
115 Nantucket Cove
San Rafael, CA 94901
415-459-3665

Provident Financial
3525 Del Mar Hts. Road, #459
San Diego, CA 92130
619-793-0086

CENTRAL REGION
Burgess and Associates
8368 South 3375 East
Salt Lake City, UT 84121
801-944-8594
Denver office: 303-607-9879

Great Plains Trading Company
3406 South 102nd Street
Omaha, NE 68124
402-393-5699

MID-WEST REGION
Harvest Commodity Brokers
1135 Kristin Drive
Libertyville, IL 60048
708-247-0023

Quantum Brokers
26411 24-Mile Road
Chesterfield, MI 48051
810-949-4058

Raimondina & Associates
3386 Arbor Way
Westlake, OH 44145
216-899-7972

EASTERN REGION
Nadherny & Glennon
8 Faneuil Hall Marketplace
Boston, MA 02109
1-800-884-6694
Offices: Connecticut, New York, New Jersey, Pennsylvania, Virginia, Maryland, North Carolina, South Carolina, Georgia

North American Commodities
184 Morgan Avenue
East Haven, CT 06512
203-466-1115

SOUTHEASTERN REGION
Southeast Market Brokerage
11831 Kingston Pike, Suite 124
Knoxville, TN 37922
1-800-789-4350

Golden Dome Commodities
1115 Executive Cove Road
Jacksonville, FL 32259
904-287-5788

Index

AAN (American Association of
    Nurserymen), 26, 45
Abandon, 173
Acer, common names, 27
Acer palmatum, growth pattern,
    119
Acer palmatum atropurpureum,
    growth pattern, 119
Acer palmatum dissectum, growth
    pattern, 120
American Association of
    Nurserymen (AAN), 26, 45
American options, 52
American Standard for Nursery
    Stock (ASNS), 45
Ask, 183
ASNS (American Standard for
    Nursery Stock), 45
Asset
    convenience, 111
    pure, 111
Assignment, 183
Associate member(ship), 183
At the money, 130, 174

Basis, 75, 184
    calculating, 75–77
    cash prices and, 82–83

hedge and, 90–92
local, importance of, 79
location and, 77–78
passage of time and, 78
predicted, 81–82
strong, 83
Basis charts, 80–81
Basis points, 80–81
Basis records, 80
Basis risk, 82, 98, 184
Bearish, 184
Bid, 184
Black and Scholes's formula,
    145–147
Botanical tree names, 27
Brand recognition, 23–24
Break-even point, 174
Broker, 184
Bullish, 184
Buyers, 43, 184
    limited risk for, 64
Buying
    call options, 151–155
    put options, 160–164

Call options, 48–49, 184
    buying, 151–155
    selling, 155–159

Call writing
   covered, 156–159, 176
   uncovered, 159–160
Calls. *See* Call options
Cancellation conditions, 5
Carrying charges, 97, 184
Carrying costs, 75
Cash account, 185
Cash flow flexibility, 50
Cash market, 67, 185
   local, 67–68
   shorting the, 154
   strong versus weak, 101
Cash market alternatives, 68–71
Cash prices, basis and, 82–83
Cash sales, 69
Cash trades, 33
CBOT (Chicago Board of
   Trade), 17
Cercidiphyllum, common
   names, 27
Cercidiphyllum japonicum,
   growth pattern, 120
Certificateless trading, 52
CFTC (Commodity Futures
   Trading Commission), 18
Charter member(ship), 185
Chicago Board of Trade
   (CBOT), 17
Class of options, 185
Clearinghouse, 43, 185
Closed harvest period, 185
Closing purchase, 185
Closing sale, 185
Closing transactions, 52–53
CNS (continuous net
   settlement), 62
Commercial hedger, 185
Commercial paper (CP), 151
Commission broker, 186
Commissions, 56, 186
Commodities, 186
   traded, 37
   transformable, 117–118
Commodity codes, 27, 28
Commodity exchanges, 35–38
   U.S., 37
Commodity Futures Trading
   Commission (CFTC), 18
Common tree names, 27

Competitive delivery, 95
Computer trading, 186
Continuous net settlement
   (CNS), 62
Contract growing, 70
Contract month, 186
Contract performance,
   guaranteed, 43–48
Contract prices, forward,
   100–101
Contract pricing, forward,
   107–108
Contract settlement, 61–63
Contract specifications, 186
Contracts, 186
   limited, 57
   option. *See* Option contracts
Convenience asset, 111
Convenience value, 111–117
Convergence, 78
Convergence interaction, 128
Cost reduction, 4
Cost understating, 97
Cost-plus pricing strategy, 67–68
Covered call writing, 156–159,
   186
Covered put writing, 165, 186
Covered writing, 187
CP (commercial paper), 151
Cumulative basis components, 75

Delayed pricing, 70–71
Delivery, 62, 187
Delivery periods, 79
Delta, 143, 187
Demand, 102–103, 187
Deposit money, 12
Derivative, 187
Disclosure document, 56
Distant forward contract
   months, 79
Distribution channels, 28
Documentation, exchange, 25

Eastern market, 98–99
Established price lists, 69
European trade centers, 31
European-style option, 52, 187
Even basis, 187
Exchange documentation, 25

Exchange-traded options, 24–28
Exchanges, 33, 187
  commodity. *See* Commodity
    exchanges
Exercise, 187
Exercise price, 58, 60, 127
Expiration
  options' value at, 129–131
  time remaining until, 134,
    140
Expiration dates, 50, 188
Expiration process, 57–58

Fagus, common names, 27
Fagus sylvatica, growth pattern,
  121
Fagus sylvatica riversi, growth
  pattern, 121
Field inspection for delivery on
  forward contracts, 45, 48
Fixed basis components, 75
Forecasting forward prices,
  107–124
Forward contract months,
  distant, 79
Forward contract prices,
  100–101
Forward contract pricing,
  107–108
Forward contracts, 49–50, 188
  field inspection for delivery on,
    45, 48
  option pricing and, 129–133
  sample, 59
  underlying, 58
Forward market performance, 95
Forward markets, 5, 10, 17, 24–25
Forward price analysis, 95–99
Forward price determination, 95
Forward prices
  forecasting, 107–124
  volatility of underlying,
    135–136
Fundamental analysis, 95
Fundamental no-arbitrage
  equation, 108–111
Future (forward) price, 188
Futures contracts, 188
  development of, 34–38
Futures (forward) market, 188

Futures trading, progression of,
  31–33

Garden centers, 96
Genera selection, 22–23
Global Exchange (GLOBEX), 42
Glossary, 183–194
Grading method, 188
Growers, 189
  smaller versus larger, 8
Growing, contract, 70
Guaranteed contract
  performance, 43–48

Hedge, 24, 87, 189
  basis and, 90–92
  lifting, 89–90, 189
  purpose of, 87–89

In the money, 130, 189
Intrinsic value, 129, 133–134,
  189
Introducing broker, 189
Inventories, 114, 116
Inventory storage, 117
Inverted markets, 100

Landscape tree production,
  26, 28
Lapsed option, 189
Letter of credit, 189
Lettres de faire, 32–33
Leverage, 49, 63–64
Lifting a hedge, 89–90, 189
Limit order, 189
Limited contracts, 57
Limited risk for buyers, 64
Liquidambar, common names, 27
Liquidambar styraciflua, growth
  pattern, 122
Local cash market, 67–68
Local cash price, 190
Local market alternatives, 68
Location
  affecting returns, 101–104
  basis and, 77–78
Long, 190
Long position, 55
Long-term options, 50

Margin account, 61
Mark-up, 190
Markdown, 190
Market fairs, 32
Market maker, 190
Market order, 190
Market performance, forward, 95
Market size, 26, 28
Markets, 190
    forward. *See* Forward markets
    inverted, 100
    secondary, 25
    for speculating, 92
    term, 24
Material, 190
Material appreciation, 75, 97
Material prices, 116
Material storage, 116–117
Member grower, 190
Mercantile law, 32
Minimum lots, 50

90/10 strategy, 151–152
Naked writing, 190
National Computerized Trading
    System (NCTS), 41
Nearby basis, 190
Net holder, 53, 55
Net writer, 55
NMR (nursery material receipt),
    44, 46–47, 191
No-arbitrage equation,
    fundamental, 108–111
Non–full-carry market, 112
Northwest market, 98–99
Nursery material receipt (NMR),
    44, 46–47, 191
Nursery materials forward
    markets, 24–25
Nursery stock, 8
Nursery stock grading standards,
    44–45
Nursery stock pricing, 4

OAN (Oregon Association of
    Nurserymen), 7
Offsetting position, 191
Open harvest period, 191
Open interest, 52, 191
Open sale, 191

Open-out cry, 41
Opening purchase, 191
Option contract size, 50–51
Option contracts, 53–64
    sample, 54
Option money, 12
Option orders, placing, 55–56
Option positions, 52
Option premium, 127
    calculating, 131–132
    establishing, 127–128
Option premium determination
    case study, 136–140
Option premium distribution, 61
Option pricing, forward
    contracts and, 129–133
Option pricing models, 140–145
Option program, 16
Option trading, volume of, 36
Option trading approach, 9
Option value, 132
Options, 24, 169, 191
    American and European styles
        of, 52–53
    benefits of, 25
    class of, 53, 185
    exchange-traded, 24–28
    exercising, 56–57
    flexibility of, 51–52
    history of, 31
    as price equalizers, 127
    types of, 48–52
    value at expiration, 129–131
    versatility of, 151
Oregon Association of
    Nurserymen (OAN), 7
Out of the money, 130, 191
Over basis, 192

Picea, common names, 27
Picea pugens, growth pattern,
    122
Picea pugens glauca, growth
    pattern, 123
Pinus, common names, 27
Pinus sylvestris, growth pattern,
    123
Pinus thunbergii, growth pattern,
    124
Points, 50

Pool, 43, 192
Position, 192
Premium, 192
Prepurchase agreement, 70
Price analysis, forward, 95–99
Price determination, forward, 95
Price discounting, 8
Price discovery, 35
Price equalizers, options as, 127
Price increases, 4
Price lists, established, 69
Price mark-up, 67
Price-discovery mechanism, 10
Price-level risk, 192
Prices, forecasting forward, 107–124
Pricing
    delayed, 70–71
    scavenger, 71
Pricing factors, 140
Pricing summary, 136
Primary market, 192
Production, usage and, 113
Purchase orders, 49
Pure asset, 111
Put options, 48–49, 192
    buying, 160–164
    selling, 164–165
Put writing
    covered, 165, 187
    uncovered, 165–166
Puts. See Put options

Retailers, 6–7
Returns, location affecting, 101–104
Risk, 4–5
    basis, 82, 98, 184
    limited, for buyers, 64
    managing, 18
    shifting of, 9, 10
Root codes and forms, 27

Scavenger pricing, 71
Seattle Mercantile Exchange (SME)
    beginning of, 11–20
    competition and, 5
    computerized trading at, 41–42

implementing, 20–22
long-term quest, 23
national member broker network, 18–19
purpose of, 3
short-term goal, 23
SEC (Securities and Exchange Commission), 18
Secondary markets, 25, 192
Securities and Exchange Commission (SEC), 18
Sellers, 43, 192
Selling
    call options, 155–159
    put options, 164–165
Series, 193
Settlement, 55, 193
    contract, 61–63
Settlement date, 193
Short, 193
Short position, 55, 89
Shorting the cash market, 154
SME. See Seattle Mercantile Exchange
Special contracts, 57
Specialty department, 193
Speculating, markets for, 92
Spot market, 67
Spot market price, 115
Spread, 97, 193
Stock options, 36
Stop limit order, 193
Stop order, 193
Storage, 69–70, 193
    inventory, 117
    material, 116–117
Strategies, 169
Strengthening, 193
Strike price, 50, 58, 60, 127, 193–194
Strong basis, 83
Supply, 194

Technical analysis, 95
TFT (trade for trade), 62
Ticker symbols, 27
Time value, 133–134, 194
"To arrive" contracts, 35
Track country station price, 194
Trade fairs, 32
Trade for trade (TFT), 62

Trade networks, 31
Trading accounts, 55–56
Transfer agent, 194
Transformable commodities,
    117–118, 124
Transportation costs, 101–102
Tree farm, 14–16
Tree names, common and
    botanical, 27
Tree production, landscape,
    26, 28
Trees, types of, 28
Two-state pricing, 141–145
Type, 194

Uncovered call writing, 159–160
Uncovered put writing, 165–166

Under basis, 194
Underlying, 194
Underlying instruments, 58
Understating, cost, 97
Underwriters, 43, 60–61, 194
Usage, production and, 113

Value, convenience, 111–117
Volatility, 140, 147, 194

Walker, Tom, 21
Wasting assets, 51
Weakening, 194
Weather patterns, 116
Wholesalers, 6–7